Dark Moon Wisdom, Dark Moon Power

Are you afraid of the "dark" aspects of the psyche? Most of us are. After all, darkness can represent the unknown, the mysterious, or the forbidden. Mainstream religions tell us that darkness is equivalent to evil.

Most books on spirituality avoid addressing your native darker aspects, even though it's vital that you claim your shadow self to become a whole, empowered person. In contrast, this book *embraces* the dark side of spirit, integrating it with the Dark Moon energies accessible through Witchcraft. Earth-centered spiritualities such as Witchcraft understand that the shadow is only one aspect of the whole human spirit, which is a blend of balancing energies: active and passive, masculine and feminine, and light and dark.

Dark Moon Mysteries draws on storytelling, journaling, guided imagery, ritual, and sacred artistry to help you incorporate dark energies into your spiritual life—and come to grips with the darker shades of your being.

You can never truly claim enlightenment until you also claim your darkness. Turn to face your shadow, and you will find a source of untapped power, peace, and balance.

"Tim Roderick has listened to the Sage and the Crone. 'Claim your darkness,' says he. 'Transform your light,' says she. 'Dance the power of your widdershins spiral.' We'd best listen, too, and pay heed to the wisdom in this book.

Barbara Ardinger, Ph.D.
Author of *A Woman's Book of Rituals and Celebrations*

A Book of the Month Club Selection

About The Author

Timothy Roderick is the author of *The Once Unknown Familiar*. He holds a master's degree in Clinical Psychology from Antioch University, and he is currently a psychotherapy intern in Southern California. He is a long-time initiate of an order of English Traditional Wicca. He has been a student of the occult, mysticism, and earth-centered spirituality for many years and is the founder of EarthDance Collective, a group that sponsors open rituals, classes, and workshops that promote awareness of feminist spirituality. Timothy also teaches classes that blend western psychology and native shamanic wisdom throughout California.

To Write the Author

If you wish to contact the author or would like more information about this book, please write to Timothy Roderick in care of Llewellyn Worldwide, and we will forward your request. Both the author and publisher appreciate hearing from you and learning of your enjoyment of this book and how it has helped you. Llewellyn Worldwide cannot guarantee that every letter written to the author can be answered, but all will be forwarded. Please write to:

Timothy Roderick
c/o Llewellyn Worldwide
P.O. Box 64383, Dept. K345-x, St. Paul, MN 55164-0383, U.S.A.

Please enclose a self-addressed, stamped envelope for reply or $1.00 to cover costs.
If outside the U.S.A., enclose international postal reply coupon.

Free Catalog from Llewellyn Worldwide

For more than ninety-five years Llewellyn has brought its readers knowledge in the fields of metaphysics and human potential. Learn about the newest books in spiritual guidance, natural healing, astrology, occult philosophy, and more. Enjoy book reviews, new age articles, a calendar of events, plus current advertised products and services. To get your free copy of the *Llewellyn's New Worlds of Mind and Spirit* magazine, send your name and address to:

Llewellyn's New Worlds of Mind and Spirit
P.O. Box 64383, Dept. K345-x, St. Paul, MN 55164-0383, U.S.A.

DARK MOON MYSTERIES

Dark Moon Mysteries

Wisdom, Power, and Magic of the Shadow World

Timothy Roderick

1996
Llewellyn Publications
Saint Paul, Minnesota, U.S.A. 55164-0383

FIRST EDITION
Second Printing, 1996

Cover Art by Anthony Meadows
Cover Design by Tom Grewe
Interior Art on pages 3, 15, 39, 55, 77, 87, 103, 115, 129, and 143 by Anthony Meadows
Interior Art on pages 34, 51, 110, 148, 154, 155, 156, and 163 by Anne Marie Garrison
Interior Design, Editing, and Interior Art on pages 134, 152, 153, 177, 186, 187, and 188 by Darwin Holmstrom

Library of Congress Cataloging-in-Publication Data
Roderick, Timothy. 1963–
    Dark moon mysteries : wisdom, power, and magic of the shadow world / Timothy Roderick. -- 1st ed.
        p.   cm.
    Includes bibliographical references.
    ISBN 1–56718–345–X (trade pbk.)
    1. Witchcraft. 2. Magic. 3. Ritual. 4. Shadow (Psychoanalysis)--Miscellanea. 5. Goddess religion. I. Title.
    BF1566.R59 1996
    133.4'3--dc20   96–13525
                                                                              CIP

Llewellyn Publications
A Division of Llewellyn Worldwide, Ltd.
St. Paul, Minnesota 55164-0383, U.S.A.

Contents

List of Fairy Tales

Acknowledgements

With sincere gratitude I wish to thank the following people who aided in the creation of this book. My good friend and editor, Mead Hunter, was instrumental in shaping this work into something accessible using his knowledge, skill, humor, and insight. My thanks to this High Priest and Sage who has had tremendous impact on my work both magically and professionally. Thanks to Karen Cummings, a wonderful psychotherapist who helped me sort out some psychological and magical theory. The members of Earthdance Coven, Crescent's Shadow, and Moontydes have been a great system of support during my own Dark Moon processes. Thanks to Victoria Sciarra who initially set me on the Widdershins path. Many thanks to B.T. Halphide for her eagle eye in the final editing stages. Finally, I must thank Lady Varda, a wise woman who knows the ways of the crone and who has guided me along my spiritual journey.

Also by Timothy Roderick:

The Once Unknown Familiar

Part 1

Shadows:
Dark Moon Wisdom

hag (hag) n. 1. an ugly old woman, esp. a vicious or malicious one. 2. a witch.

hagio-, a learned borrowing from Greek meaning "saint," "holy," "sacred," used in the formation of compound words: hagiology, hagiocracy.

hagiocracy (hag' e ok' r se) n. 1. government by a body of persons esteemed as holy.

—Burleigh Muten, *Word Magic*[1]

Chapter 1

The Meaning of Darkness

The Sage speaks:

I have grown old. Death speaks to my brittle bones, calling me to rejoin the Mother. Time is now my enemy, for all of the wisdom that I have gained from my arts can be lost much more easily than it was acquired. The season has come to initiate you into my secrets. I am about to give you a great gift, my beloved—the gift of darkness. You have lived with it all of your life, yet you have ignored it, feared it, shunned it, or in some way denied it. But it has never gone away; gifts from the Gods rarely do. And oh, what great treasures the dark holds—treasures beyond your imagining. Yet because these treasures are placed in chambers that you yourself lock and call forbidden, they are forgotten—but never have they been lost! Only you can unlock the chamber door. And to do this takes great courage, for when you find a keep bolted as heavily and as fast as this you know it to be shut for some good reason, eh?

3

Easily a thought can skitter across your mind when you see the gated entryway: "Some demon must lie in wait there. Whatever is in there must be dangerous or surely it would not be closed away." But remember my dear, demons exist on either side of that locked door. It is when you no longer have passage to the other side that you are truly trapped in the chamber with a dangerous thing. The key to this locked chamber lies in the arts of the dark moon.

The dark moon, the time between the full moon and the new moon, carries secrets all its own. Look to the moon as she wanes and you will find a mirror of your own inner darkness—your dark self. It is this very mystery that keeps the fainthearted at bay. It is for the better that most magical folk, and even you yourself, hesitate to fully engage in the magical crafts of the dark moon. For fear is the demon hidden away, skulking in the corners beyond the lock. Fear whispers to you—even now. It says darkness is a force beyond human control; it is best kept dormant.

Even the cowan[2] folk not drawn to the Lady's ways, those who do not make study of her cycles, are taught to fear what they call "shadow." The cowans and their priests talk of darkness as though it was their "satan," or fear it as a realm of devils. But, thinking on it, in some strange way, they know of what they speak. For one great secret of darkness is this: fear locked away in the shadows turns into an endlessly tormenting devil. Ah, but face the dark and you will find a place of untapped power, rest, peace, harmony, and finally, balance. To the wise adept, to the brave adept, an exploration into the cave of darkness yields the jewels of knowledge and wisdom (beyond that which is already known). It is the sacred ground where destiny changes. Your destiny changes there, my child.

The dark brings change. It reveals what was once thought forbidden in knowledge. I remember a time not so long ago that the cowans named my beloved crafts, the crafts of magic, the crafts of the Wicca, "black arts," black signifying the forbidden. Those who dared not go beyond the light places named it thusly. Oh, the light places are not to be scorned, mind you, for the light too holds great power. However, without shadow, light cannot be seen.

Look here: a shadow is darkness, is it not? Tell me this: when you stand in sunlight and you see your shadow, do you fear its presence? Of course you do not! Yet, the shadow is the very likeness of you in an image of darkness. You must learn to dance with your shadow as you have learned to dance with the sunlight.

If you peer too long into the light of the sun, the brightest light we know of, darkness is all you'll ever see after that. Ah, but peer

into the darkest of darkness and you'll begin to see more deeply. You will begin to see other realities and hidden worlds.

Darkness is never far away, either. Close your eyes, my dear, and you are already there in its sweet, soft silence.

The Meaning of Darkness

Who's afraid of the dark? Few would readily admit to such a thing. But if the exterior of our personalities could be removed like a mask, underneath we would all find a part of us that is resistant to darkness—maybe even a little afraid of it. This is a perfectly natural response. I was afraid of it too. However, it is ridiculous to stick our heads in the sand and hide from reality. Darkness exists all around us—on more than one level.

Of course, darkness manifests on the material level. The sun goes down, the stars appear and the physical reality of darkness, the blackness of the universe, opens before us nightly. But the work of the mystic, the work in which you are about to engage, is to see beyond gross physical reality. If you shift your perspective slightly and imagine that the physical reality that you observe right now illustrates metaphorically what is going on within you, you will see that inner darkness is a natural, spiritual state that simply exists, like the blackness of space. It is nothing to fear. It simply is. And awareness of this darkness waxes and wanes like the light of the moon or like the rising and setting of the sun.

But what is this darkness?

In the course of this book, you will be taking a journey into the innermost recesses of the human spirit. On the way you will learn that "darkness" is a multilayered term that holds a variety meanings. For instance, to those mystics who tread the path beyond the light, the dark represents the unknown. They know that they have arrived in the shadowlands when they are faced with exploring wisdom, knowledge, and power that feels out of bounds or unsafe—not because the dark actually is unsafe, but because our culture tells us it is so. In another aspect, the Dark is what you don't want to see within yourself. It is what psychologists call "the shadow" part of your consciousness.[3]

Although darkness can feel menacing, it is not a place of utter dread. After all, when it gets dark enough, you can see the stars, and stars, in this case, are your points of brilliance. The dark is a place full of paradox; the fear you may have once felt transforms into strength and wisdom once you face darkness and assimilate it into your being. You will find that although Western, monotheistic culture equates the term *dark* with "evil," people with an earth-centered spiritual view see darkness in a completely different way. They see it as only one half of the total human spirit, which is a mix of active and passive, male and female, light and dark energy, as symbolized by the familiar yin-yang symbol from Asia. The journey into the dark can help you to reconstruct and complete your power as a human being, as a mixture of both positive and negative, constructive and destructive, active and passive power.

Even pure, white light is made up of many colors in combination—some of which are dark and invisible to the naked eye. If you understand that, metaphorically, this continuum of light exists within us all, then you can never really claim enlightenment until you claim your darkness. Coming to grips with these darker shades of your being is an act of personal empowerment. Once you accept the reality of darkness in your life, you open up your consciousness. You widen your personal spectrum and finally you emerge into full light.

When you refuse to see life in any other way than that which reveals all aspects—light, dark, and everything in between—then you are doing something dangerous. You are acting counterculturally. In that instant, you are taking a stand against the limited and insipid ways of existing in the world up to that point.

That is not to say the spiritual journey you have taken up to now has been useless, for it has prepared you and led you to the point of readiness to face your darkness. The fact that you are here at the start of this process shows that all spiritual paths converge at the crossroads of truth. But the culturally acceptable spiritual paths (mainstream religions, for example) typically do not encourage a close look at the dark. This is even true for the numerous popular "new age" paths that purvey "white light" and positive affirmations as panaceas for scattering all manner of dark apparitions.

There is a certain sophistry evident in such paths. While they may seem convincing and fulfilling at first, they may leave you feeling as though you can never be a perfect being, because human experience and common sense show you that you can't hold on to the white light forever. Nobody can. The world we live in is not complete happiness, rainbows, sunshine, and unicorns. The search for happiness and the search for perfection are two separate courses.

Happiness is a frame of mind that you can strive toward and attain. Perfection is your *natural* state of being. It is where you are and how you are right now: mad, sad, glad, afraid, or neutral. This is a difficult lesson to accept because most Western religions have taught us that perfection is something unattainable on Earth. Because of this, you may think that your personal darkness is somehow a mistake—it is something that takes you away from "perfection"—so you muffle it. You hide it. You try to keep it out of sight—and out of mind. But in our mystical, earth-centered (or pagan) definition of perfection, darkness is actually a part of it.

The spiritual work ahead has nothing to do with scattering darkness; if you scatter the darkness, you scatter a part of your very being. The work of the dark moon mysteries has to do with confronting darkness, learning from it, and assimilating it.

Most of us have never considered a journey into our darkness because we actively mute our inner voice each time it calls us to the path, every time we face a painful moment or an instance of emotional darkness. However, a muted inner voice is not a self-empowered one; self-empowerment is the path of the mystical pagan. Once you deviate from self-empowerment, it is a sign that you have disengaged from your inner voice, your source of intuition. Once that happens you hand your power over to the rest of the world and look to others for leadership, guidance, salvation.[4]

The real work of journeying into the dark involves looking inward and discovering your own voice, your own guidance, and your own power.

AN INVITATION TO THE DARK

Change and transition are the essence of darkness. The term *essence* is emphasized here because essences are themselves keys to unlocking the secrets of the dark moon mysteries. Distilling complex concepts, mystical revelations, and magical wisdom into their essences is an important task in any spiritual endeavor. When an idea is distilled into its essence, it becomes a symbol. Symbols, essences, principles, and experiences that have universal meaning are called archetypes. Another way of describing an archetype is to call it a motif, a basic pattern that repeats itself among many disparate cultures and in many various guises.[5] Archetypes are found in abundance within any culture's folklore or mythology—two genres of storytelling that often reveal significant mystical insights.

In European culture, the contemporary form that this mystical folklore takes is the fairy tale. Many of the tales with which we are most familiar have been in existence from time immemorial and were, at one time, stories retold by the village wise woman or man,[6] the priest or priestess of the earth religions prevalent in "Old Europe" (Europe prior to the coming of the Romans and the Christians).[7]

There are two archetypal figures from myth and fairy tale that symbolize change, transition, and darkness. The Crone (the hag, the woman past childbearing years), for instance, is the archetype for women's dark power.[8] She appears in forms such as the entombed mother, the lady of the tree in the tale of "Ashputtel," who provides guidance and magical aid.[9] She often appears as a good fairy, such as in the tale of "Briar Rose."[10] In another aspect, the Crone can be the bearer of justice, like the old enchantress of "Rapunzel."[11]

For men, the repeated motif is that of the Sage or the hermit, the male no longer preoccupied by sexuality or by hunting pursuits.[12] He is the male turned inward. He appears in "The Three Heads of the Well" as the wise old man of the cave who directs the magical journey of those traveling the road.[13] As the mystical harper of "Binnorie," he appears in his aspect of the bearer of justice.[14] In the tale of "Childe Rowland," the Sage assumes a role that is the counterpart of the wise and benevolent fairy godmother or good fairy.[15]

Together, the Crone and Sage teach the way of return, the way of the widdershins (or "counterclockwise") spiral. This spiral is a symbol for the dark moon cycle of life that whirls you out of physical being, physical manifestation, and action. It swirls you toward your spiritual center, where you encounter inward being, manifestation, and action. The Crone and Sage help you to infuse every physical action with meaning, which turns every movement in your life into something sacred.

The spiritual path called Wicca is one that resonates with and embraces the archetypes of darkness. The path of the Wicca is also called Witchcraft. The word itself may be startling to some readers and amusing to others. Most of us think of witches as shadowy beings—old, ugly hags bent over bubbling cauldrons. What other personifications do we really believe in, other than those promulgated by mass culture? Beyond the myths and legends lies the reality of the Witch's tradition, which focuses on honoring and affirming the relationship between human beings, the divine, and power.

Those focal points of the Witch's sacred life are the same for all who are engaged in a shamanic spiritual path. Shamanic traditions are those that evoke a part of women and men that is natural, primal and wild. A shaman is a person in a tribal culture who confronts the world of the supernatural. To most people, the word *shaman* means "medicine man" or "medicine woman." A shaman is a learned one, a healer, a priestess or priest, a wise one. No matter which culture the shaman appears in, his or her main work is that of encountering spiritual powers and then harnessing them for some use. It is these same indigenous, shamanic practices of the earth-honoring religions of Northern and Western Old Europe that comprise the basis of the tradition called Wicca. In other words, Witches are shamans.

Whether we've read the fairy tales, seen movies, or just listened to a good story about Witches, we all know that they are beings who dare to do what no one else would. They know things no one else knows. They venture beyond the village compound, beyond cultural norms, values, and strictures. They move beyond the realm of the known. It is exactly there that they find such things as truth and empowerment for themselves. Truth for the Witch is self-knowledge. Empowerment for the Witch comes from magic.

Magic is another word that may raise an eyebrow or two, but in spiritual work magic has nothing to do with trickery. It is a method that Witches use to unite with the flow of spiritual power. One of the better definitions of magic is "the ability to change consciousness at will."[16] Once a Witch has complete self-knowledge, her consciousness has changed and magic is in the air.

Risking a journey into your own darkness is a Witch's or shaman's journey because it takes you beyond the known as well. The journey changes your consciousness because along the way you encounter all that seems unsafe, ugly, and unknown about yourself. It also pushes through the bounds of what you define as power. But the magic comes when you are able to transform that internal darkness into light by pulling up the material that once resided solely in dark, unconscious places and making it conscious. This is done by spiraling inward, widdershins, honoring your inner voice, your inner movement, your personal points of growth, and reclaiming your own power.

Witches do not claim their power from darkness, as the dominant culture tells us. Witches claim their power through darkness. The word is an active one, and it implies that Witches actively pursue their power; it is not a manifestation of some external source. They honor their *power from within*.[17]

When your inner voice gives you an invitation into the dark places, it is time to evoke the Witch's power to dare and claim your own power through darkness. This is a call to summon your own inner strength, and then move into action. When darkness calls to you, it is really inviting you to act in self-empowered ways, just like Witches and shamans.

In significant ways, your journey into darkness is the journey toward becoming the archetype of the Witch, the Sage, the Crone, the wise man, the hag, the being of magic, the being of power. But above all, the journey into darkness is about coming to terms with your wholeness, completion, and perfection.[18] One perceptive and useful observation from Eastern mysticism is that everything in the Universe is one. When you accept this premise, then you realize that you cannot be whole when you focus on the light and ignore the dark.

The invitation to darkness is mutual; it beckons to you, but you too must beckon. It is important to yearn for wholeness and completion before you engage in the work of darkness. The moment you engage the dark, you embark on a pathway that can lead to its resolution.

Shadows can control every move that you make without your ever knowing, which is one of the aspects worth resolving. It has masterful control of you because the more you monitor and rigorously suppress your shadowy self-aspects, the more it controls how you can act. For instance, you can't be sad, cry, be angry, or show aggressiveness, so you stay in control of what you can say and do. You spend time continually swerving around road cones instead of driving straight on ahead.

However, you can learn from shadow and gain power through it by recognizing those dark moon aspects of yourself—the hidden, the unknown, the unexplored, even the unspeakable—and begin to move toward them and through them, as do shamans and Witches. In doing this, you rob the darkness of any power it held over you and a marvelous transformation takes place.

From observation, it would seem that the darkness becomes light. However, it is your internal locus that shifts. It is not the light that transforms—you do. Through this work with darkness, you can then see that it is really is an aspect of light, that the dark is one of light's many shadings.

The Sage speaks:

Ask yourself this: what good is it to live eternally in the light? One of light's aspects is exposing that which is already known, that which is obvious and mundane. Remember, my clever one, that life forms wither and die when left to bask in too much light. Darkness maintains balance within the web of life.

Now let me tell you what was told to me when I was a young apprentice. Without darkness to balance out the light, there can be no natural growth, change, or transformation. All in the light is in its perfection. All that is in the dark is in its perfection as well.

This is what I know: light and dark are qualities that we humans have agreed mean something. I mean that we have embellished these words so that their meanings feel solid and real. The illusion of words is enticing, but in the end, they are merely puffs of air to which we assign worth. The only worth these words have lies in their ability to describe varied aspects of the same energy: that of the Gods.

Night comes upon day as quickly as does winter upon summer. When you reflect on the cycles of nature and her seasons you can plainly see that the Gods do not spare us from equal durations of darkness and light. Neither the Winter nor nighttime is but a brief instant, now, is it? One season flows into the next with ease. Day flows into night without hesitation or fear. Why then should you fear the darkness within yourself? It is merely an extension of nature's cycles. See here: darkness is an aspect of light.

Our Great Goddess, as you know, has three faces or aspects, if you like. She appears as the Maiden, the Mother, or the Crone. The Maiden can be seen as a light aspect of the Goddess, the Crone is her dark aspect, and the Mother is her aspect which hangs somewhere in the balance. If you were to acknowledge each of her aspects in turn and work with the power of each of her faces evenly through the course of your magical studies, one third of your spiritual journey would be centered around the mysteries of darkness. But you knew that already, didn't you?

Energy—no matter what its form—never goes away; this you must know well. Therefore, if you neglect either light or dark energy, it builds up. It gains muscle and begins to dominate your life. Mirror the balance of nature; call to your darkness, listen to it, drink deeply of it, and move through it. You cannot fully claim your power as an earth magician until you have achieved the Great Balance. This is a true secret of your magical crafts, of your Wicca-crafts, my dearest.

LEAVING THE LIGHT

Your journey into the dark will be divided into three sections: Shadows, Spirals, and Spells.

In section one, "Shadows," you will encounter the personal realm of darkness. You will confront the shadow self, an elusive and often troublesome aspect of spirit. This part of the journey will follow the structure of a myth, and focus particularly on the heroine's or hero's journey within a mythic structure.

Myths, folklore, and fairy tales originate from the same zone as dreams, those potent nightly phantasms that bespeak the promptings of our unconscious life.[19] Myths, folklore, and fairy tales can be metaphors, guides, and even maps for journeying through the unconscious, which is a vast reservoir of nonlinear thought, creativity and inner power that taps both light and dark.

Noted scholar of mythology, Joseph Campbell, divides this journey into three distinct parts, each of which translates into a task: "The Call to Adventure," "Crossing the Threshold," and "Return."[20] Through these tasks, you will confront the shadow, gain its wisdom and power, and then assimilate it, using fairy tales, journaling, guided imagery, sacred artistry, and ritual.

In section two, "Spirals," you will learn of the second half—the dark half—of the "spiral dance," which I call the widdershins spiral. This work unleashes your "dark" energy. Widdershins energy is that which spirals you inward to the core of your sacred self to touch the very source of power. In this section you will journey through "reverse" powers and attributes of the four symbolic, magical compass directions—west, south, east, and north—and you will learn how to incorporate these energies into your spiritual life. Again, I will use fairy tales to illustrate points, and you will be guided through sacred imagery and power exercises to activate your dark power.

Section three, "Spells," is a grimoire of enchantments, charms, and other magical workings that will put your newly activated dark moon power to use.

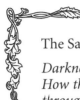

The Sage speaks:

Darkness has no preferences, nor has it any feelings or emotions. How the darkness must wonder at those of us who tread lightly through its passages. I can teach you how to move through the darkness—and before long, you will dance through it. To crawl through darkness denotes fear; to dance through it signifies power.

Come! I will point the way to your wisdom and teach you of the full range of your power. I will look for you soon, when the moon begins to wane. We have a long journey ahead, my dear. The darkness awaits!

Notes

1. Burleigh Muten, *Word Magic*, copyright 1993 Burleigh Muten.

2. *Cowan* is a word used by Priests and Priestesses of Wicca to indicate non-initiates.

3. C. G. Jung, R.F.C. Hull (trans.), Joseph Campbell (ed.), *The Portable Jung*, New York: Viking Press, 1971, p. 145.

4. Sonia Johnson, *Going Out of Our Minds: The Metaphysics of Liberation*, Freedom: Crossing Press, 1987, p. iii.

5. C. G. Jung, *Man and His Symbols*, New York: Doubleday, 1964, pp. 67–68.

6. Jack Zipes, (trans.), *Beauties, Beasts and Enchantment: Classic French Fairy Tales*, New York: Meridian, 1991, pp. 1–2.

7. Marija Gimbutas, *Gods and Goddesses of Old Europe*, Los Angeles: University of California Press, 1982, p. 17.

8. C. G. Jung, *Man and His Symbols*, New York: Doubleday, 1964, p. 196.

9. The Brother's Grimm, *Fairy Tales*, New York: Alfred A. Knopf, 1992, pp. 214–222.

10. The Brother's Grimm, *Fairy Tales*, New York: Alfred A. Knopf, 1992, pp. 41–47.

11. The Brother's Grimm, *Fairy Tales*, New York: Alfred A. Knopf, 1992, pp. 95–100.

12. C. G. Jung, *Man and His Symbols*, New York: Doubleday, 1964, p. 196.

13. Joseph Jacobs, *English Folk and Fairy Tales*, (3rd edition, revised), New York: G. P. Putnam's Sons, (n.d.) pp. 232–237.

14. Joseph Jacobs, *English Folk and Fairy Tales*, (3rd edition, revised), New York: G. P. Putnam's Sons, (n.d.) pp. 42–47.

15. Joseph Jacobs, *English Folk and Fairy Tales*, (3rd edition, revised), New York: G. P. Putnam's Sons, (n.d.) pp. 122–129.

16. Quoted by Starhawk, in *The Spiral Dance*, San Francisco: HarperCollins, 1989.

17. Starhawk, *Truth or Dare*, San Francisco: Harper & Row, 1987, p. 23.

18. Jacqueline Small, *Awakening in Time*, New York: Bantam Books, 1991, pp. 43–44.

19. M. Masud R. Khan, "The Changing Use of Dreams in Psychoanalytic Practice," *International Journal of Psycho-Analysis*, (1976) 57, p. 328.

20. Joseph Campbell, *The Hero With A Thousand Faces*, "Part I: The Adventure of the Hero," New Jersey: Princeton University Press, 1969, pp. 8–10.

Chapter 2

Naming the Shadow

The Sage speaks:

See there—up in the heavens she wanes! The crone moon removes her mask of light. She reveals her mysteries for all.

What is your mask? Did you know that you wear one, my beloved? And what is it that lies beneath? In my time, I have worn a great many masks: large and small, ornate and stark. Each mask revealed as much as it concealed. I learned well that there are times when masks should and should not be worn.

It is easy to become bound by the illusion of the masks we wear when we live in the belief that there is nothing beneath the mask. It is then that we treasure it beyond its worth.

It is natural to wear a mask. It is when you think you do not wear one that the masquerade becomes a dangerous exercise. The masks you will sense the least are those of your darkness. This is because you are taught by your elders and by those of the village to shun the presence of these masks. What's more, the village folk say to you, "do not point to the dark masks of others." So you sleep and forget and lose the wisdom and power of these masks.

What madness this is. We see each other's masks of darkness as clearly as though they were our own. We learn not to tell the emperor that he is naked, and in the process we pretend we are fully clothed as well.

I now say to you: know your masks well, my wise one, see them in detail and name them, each one.

Introduction to Shadow Work

When the moon begins to wane, the darkness that you see cast across her face is a shadow. This moon-shadow is a potent symbol for the darkness that manifests on the personal, spiritual level. *Shadow* is an element of human consciousness that is made up of significant fears, memories, emotions, and experiences that, over the course of your life, you have rejected in some way or held back from flooding into your full waking consciousness. For example, when you have an emotional response to something, but decide to ignore that emotion, it gets stuffed into a dark corner of your consciousness where it becomes a part of your shadow.[1]

Let's say you go strolling down the sidewalk, when suddenly from twenty yards behind you you hear the sound of squealing car brakes and then a prodigious crash! You turn to see an automobile wrapped around a telephone pole. From where you are standing, you can see the driver slumped over the steering wheel. You feel frozen; your heart is the only thing that moves and you can feel it pounding in your throat. Within seconds, other people are on the scene helping the driver out of the car. An ambulance arrives and takes the injured party away. Someone on the sidewalk notices the drawn expression on your face, approaches you and says, "Are you all right?" You put on the best smile that you can and say, "Sure, I'm fine." You may feel like crying. You may feel shock or horror. But you hold it in, for whatever reason. That held-in experience has been stuffed away and will soon became a part of your shadow.

The shadow is the emotional part of you that you either don't want to look at or cannot look at. When you are forced into confronting it you feel uncomfortable, yet it is an essential part of human makeup.

You wouldn't be human without a shadow. But in our culture there exists an unspoken agreement among us all not to look at it. You don't look at my shadow, I won't look at yours, and nobody should ever look at their own! This kind of collusion perpetuates an unhealthy (and absolutely unnecessary) fear of darkness.[2]

This fear is reinforced everywhere: in mainstream religions, in the media, in our families, on the streets, in schools.[3] This pervasive inculcation keeps every one of us in a reactive mode and keeps shadow at arms-length at all times. It keeps us taking the long route around the dark forest, rather than the short one that goes directly through to the desired destination.

Contemporary earth-centered spiritual paths go against the grain of mainstream fear of darkness. The mystics on these paths—*neopagans,* as they are called—do not promulgate the notion that humans are born inherently wrong, bad, or evil simply because they have a shadow. That idea is left to the contemporary monotheistic religions and their followers. Neopagans feel the shadow is a natural part of the human psyche and spirit that, if allowed to unfold, becomes a great teacher and a source of power. It may feel like a momentous task to override cultural inculcation. But in order to experience a change in consciousness, the first assignment of the neopagan, shaman, or Witch is to become aware of and eventually create a sense of personal detachment from such social strictures. This will be your task as well, as you follow along this course of study. Over time you will see that the social codes governing behavior and belief are simply masks that can be easily worn or discarded at will. But before that can happen, it always feels as though the masks are a living part of the *face,* or presentation to the world. It feels like there is nothing underneath. It feels as though the mask is all there is.

Once you begin to pry loose the cultural masks you wear, you can see your true face shining beneath the culturally constructed one. That fresh face will always include those dark, shadow-self aspects. The thought of exploring in such a way may send some readers into a panic. They may set this book on their shelves and dread ever seeing its pages again.

Confronting the shadow, contemplating its meaning, and assimilating its power is an initiatory journey into the earth-life of your spirit well worth taking. It is the shadow that calls for resolution so that your spirit can evolve. Each of us is called to master our old lessons so that we can effectively handle new ones. Working with the shadow in Western cultures is an acquired skill. We need to adapt to darkness just as we would to a new environment.

The shadow demands from you change, growth, and development.[4] What makes most people uncomfortable about facing a time of change is the fact that it involves a death and a rebirth—death of an old way of being, behaving, and perceiving, and the rebirth of a new way. Death and rebirth are the two core motifs of spiritual initiation rites in cultures all over the globe. Indeed, your exploration of the shadow is a journey into self-initiation. It is an initiation into the power of being fully human.

Through this shadow initiation, you face a type of death because you begin to remove yourself from the cycle of personal illusion. By this I mean that once you accept those dark, shadowy parts of your being, you can no longer live your life wearing only the masks the culture expects you to wear. Embracing the shadow is the work of embracing your truth, accepting your life for what it really is—a mix of joy and pain, light and dark. It is also the work of accepting yourself for who you really are, and honoring those parts that you think are good, as well as those parts you think are less than honorable. When you reject the path of shadow, you reject a part of yourself; you censor and deny that which could bring you into your full human power. The final outcome of this journey toward assimilating the shadow is a rebirth to wholeness, internal balance, and natural perfection.

Shadows can be either a blessing or a curse, and *you* control which they will be. Once you assimilate them into your psyche, shadows no longer feel threatening; you become more magically powerful and you begin to feel spiritual liberation. Shadows are blessings because they stretch you in new directions; they stimulate growth and self-awareness. A vast amount of blocked psychic energy rushes through you once shadows are looked at, accepted, and named for what they are[5]— aspects of a continuum of light. If left unattended, they are a curse, for they can ultimately drain you of energy, life, and wisdom.

The Spectrum of Shadow

Shadow has a spectrum, just as does light. The shadow spectrum is divided into two main categories: upper and lower shadow, or as I call them, the *shadow mask* and *subshadow*. Again, as with the spectrum of light, the shadow mask and subshadow are melded together. Sometimes it is difficult to know where one ends and the other begins. The shadow mask is any dark behavior or action. Into this category fall those behaviors that are visibly detrimental and injurious to yourself or to others. The shadow mask is a behavior that could be recorded if you were followed by a video camera. It is a manifestation of some unresolved, blocked, past emotional event. The blocked part of your spirit that continues to go unresolved is called the subshadow. The subshadow is like a mood that fuels the shadowy behavior.

Most of us have more than one visible shadow mask, but some shadows are more prominent than others. Sometimes you mistakenly feel you are concealing these masks from the gaze of others. More often you are merely concealing them from yourself. Whether or not you are conscious of wearing your shadow masks, undoubtedly you have a sense of just how ugly they can be. This usually prompts people to try to hide their shadows in earnest. However, hiding a part of you that calls for attention is not easy. In fact, attempting to hide your shadow masks causes them to emerge in an inflated way, so that no one can ignore them.[6] Trying to hide the shadow mask is like trying to submerge an inflated basketball in a pool of water. It just won't stay down.

The surest way you reveal your shadows to the world is to cast a longshadow. The *longshadow* is your own shadow lengthened and cast on to another person.[7] In other words, you ascribe your dark traits to another person.

A look into the crone and sage's cosmic mirror reveals the stark truth that darkness resides within each of us, a reality too painful for some to bear. When this darkness becomes too uncomfortable, some may try to externalize their shadow masks. Once the locus of the shadow mask is "out there," then others are viewed as bad, wrong, threatening, or in some other way shadowy.

Not only can an individual cast a longshadow, but so can groups. For example, think of the numerous religious groups that espouse a belief of love, yet hate is all that their members demonstrate. These religious groups may cast the longshadow by vilifying other belief systems. Another example is a group that may advocate peace, but which will use violent measures to keep its idea of peace in order. The members cast a longshadow when they impose the responsibility of their actions onto others who they claim provoke a violent response. These are the manifestations of the shadow mask unresolved.

The shadow mask is an aspect of your outer presentation to the rest of the world, and the good news is that like all masks, it is removable. That is to say, your behaviors can change.

Remember, a shadow mask is composed of visibly detrimental or injurious behaviors that come from unresolved emotions.[8] As an example, let us call one of your masks "argumentativeness." It is identifiable as a mask because it is a behavior, a visible part of your personality. However, argumentativeness does not have to be present in order for your personality, spirit, or power to be complete. It is not the only trait that defines you. It is simply one of the tools you may use in communication.

Because argumentativeness is a tool, you can manipulate it; you can make decisions on when to use it or not. Knowing this is vital, because it illustrates what power and versatility you have with your masks. You can decide whether or not to wear them. Once you master your masks, your presentation in life is like that of an actor in an ancient Greek play—you can "become" whatever you would like to be through the careful selection of masks.

The second shading of personal darkness, *subshadow*, points to a more challenging aspect. Subshadows are the roots of your shadow masks; they are your shadows' place of origin. Exploring this origin point of your shadow masks can be a threatening experience. It may be a memory; it may be an unconsciously recorded trauma from infancy. Whatever the specific cause, typically the subshadow's point of emergence is the past. Somewhere in the past you inherited your shadow mask—your dark behavior. No one wears masks when born. From birth, each of us acts out of pure spontaneity. But over time, it is family, friends, and the culture into which we are born that hand us the shadow masks we wear in later life.

What makes this difficult is knowing that you cannot change the past (at least not on the mundane level). The past must be accepted as a *fait accompli*. That does not mean that you are fated to merely accept and wear the masks given to you as a "done deal." Though you may be handed masks, you ultimately decide whether or not to wear them and bring them to life. Working with the subshadow is the work of freeing up the energy held captive by the past, which is the life-spring that keeps your various shadow masks alive.

When you recognize your shadowy behaviors, a window of opportunity opens for you to move into your inward life and become aware of any connected emotional responses that might have been stuffed out of sight. This is not an easy task, especially since many of us have had a lot of practice ignoring our emotions. After years of ignoring this very real part of your self-expression, you can get to the point where emotions might feel insignificant, too subtle or unimportant to deal with. The effect of this is like tightly tying a tourniquet on your arm. After a while the arm starts to lose sensation, turn blue, and die off.

The process of confronting subshadow is like taking the tourniquet off your emotions. A part of your spirit, just like the tied arm, begins to tingle, wake up, and come back to life. It is restored to the rest of your spirit so that you become whole and balanced. You begin to take off the tourniquet when you tune into your emotional responses.

When you experience an unusually strong emotional response to a person or situation, it is usually an indication that subshadow is attached. This subshadow may actually be born from an encounter with an entirely different person or situation than the one currently setting off the dark emotional response, but the current situation resembles the original experience in some aspect, so your subshadow comes forward in an effort to find resolution to the original incident.

Working with the subshadow is a long, gradual process that requires patience and practice. It is subtle but powerful dark moon work. Along the way there can be moments of psychic release from the past, but the pace that may have led to these moments can feel like that of a snail on a steep, uphill grade. In this work, it is important to keep in mind that any resolution achieved, no matter how large or small, should be attended to as though it were new root growth—tender, fragile, and in need of stimulation and nurturing. Once you have a few victories under your belt, you may discover a noticeable shift in your personal power. You will feel spiritually stronger and freer than before.

Your journey into the dark will begin with the discovery or *naming* of the shadow mask. The tales within this book illustrate the points that will follow. Here, then, is your entry way to the gated path of darkness, your first tale of shadow.

Tom Tit-Tot

Once there was a woman and her daughter who lived in a far off kingdom. Although the daughter was intelligent, fair, and charming, her mother worried that she might never marry. One day, when the girl was sixteen, her mother sat spinning a skein of yarn. As she span[9] she grumbled to herself, worrying about her daughter's plight. The king happened to be roaming through the village and passing by the cottage of the grumbling woman. The king, hearing the grumbling, wanted to know what weighed so heavily on the old woman's mind. The woman, embarrassed that the king might know her secret fear, told him that she was not actually grumbling, but telling herself how proud she was of her clever daughter who had spun five skeins of wool that very day.

Upon hearing this, the king told the mother to send her daughter to the palace where she would have everything she wanted for eleven months of a year. For repayment, in the twelfth month her daughter was expected to spin five skeins of yarn every day. If she were to do this, he would marry her.

The mother, so relieved that her daughter had married and married well, packed her bags and sent her off to live in the palace with the king. So off to the palace went the daughter, where she lived like royalty for eleven months. She had everything she could ever want during that time. On the first morning of the twelfth month, she was taken to a dark dungeon of the palace that only contained a spinning wheel and a mound of flax. Before she was locked into the dungeon, the king told her that she was to spin five skeins by nightfall or she would be beheaded.

The poor girl, left alone, wept bitterly at her plight. Just then, a small dark elf popped up through the window. He laughed and said that not only did he understand the girl's situation, but that he would help her. "I'll take the flax each morning and return with five skeins each night," he said.

Skeptical of his offer, the girl asked, "What's your pay?"

"I'll give you three guesses each night to guess my name. If you haven't guessed it by the last night, you'll be mine forever!" Since the girl really had no other choice, she reluctantly agreed and before she knew it, the tiny thing grabbed the flax and went flying out the window.

She waited and worried all day that he might not return, but that night, he came back as promised with the five skeins. "Have you guessed my name yet?" asked the imp.

The girl had been thinking of names, and she put them to the test. "Is it Jacob? How about Ned? Is it Mark?"

"No, no, and no!" screeched the elf and then he flew out the window.

Every day the tiny, dark elf would take the flax and return each night with five skeins. All day long the poor girl would try thinking of names, but she never hit the right one. Finally, on the day before the last in the month, the king came down to the basement for a visit. Since he knew that she would hold to her end of the bargain, he softened and thought to cheer her with an amusing story. "Today I had the oddest experience," said the king. "I was on a hunt when all of a sudden I heard some humming sound. I followed the noise to a great chalk pit where I saw the oddest creature. He was a tiny, dark elf who was spinning flax like mad and singing to himself: 'Nimmy nimmy not, my name's Tom Tit-Tot!'" When the girl heard this she was extremely excited, but did not say a word.

On the last evening, the tiny dark elf returned with the final five skeins. He had a malicious look in his eye. "Have you guessed my name yet?" he asked.

"Is it Sammle?" she asked.

"No," he said coming closer to her.

"Is it Zebedee?" she asked.

"No," he said coming even closer. "Take time woman, next guess and you're mine!"

The girl backed up a step or two, pointed and said, "Nimmy nimmy not, your name's Tom Tit-Tot!" With that, the imp let out a horrible shriek and flew into the dark, and she never saw it anymore.[10]

There is an old magical saying that if you know the name of something you will have power over it. This axiom is especially true when working with shadow. To be specific, once you know the name of your shadow mask, then you will have greater control of it. It won't have the ability to easily sneak up on you and play out its antics.

In practical terms this means that once you know what your shadow mask is, then you can recognize the times when you are wearing it. Once you have been made aware of the form of your shadow mask, you cannot erase the heightened consciousness achieved from that awareness. What this does is center you in your own self-knowledge. Once you know what your shadow mask *is*, you will know what it *does*. You will be able to anticipate its tricks and make conscious choices about whether or not the shadow mask is serving you and whether or not you need to wear it at any given time.

In the process of knowing the name of the shadow mask, you create magic because you have directed a change in consciousness. The shadow mask is born from an emotional entity—the subshadow. Emotions, particularly the shadowy ones, are fluid and almost vaporous in nature. When you take note of your mask, it opens the way for you to notice your emotions, or in essence, shine the light of conscious awareness on them. When this happens, they either evaporate completely or shape-shift into something entirely different.[11]

Noticing the shadow mask falls into a category of magical work that I call *naming*. Naming means specifically identifying something. Through this process of specifically identifying the shadow mask, you generate a force-field of magic.

But this isn't magic of any garden variety. The magic connected with naming the shadow mask is always transformational and life-changing. When you know the name of the shadow mask, its power over you greatly decreases, and you immediately feel the effects of its loosened grip. It may be subtle at first, but over time the effects will be an increase in your individual magical potency, as well as growth in your non-magical life. Awareness of the shadow mask frees up great quantities of magical energy that a Witch, shaman, and Priest or Priestess of the Old Ways can utilize for more positive ends.

Application of "Tom Tit-Tot"

In the story of Tom Tit-Tot we see a vivid example of the naming process between a young woman and her shadow mask. The girl is brought to the palace and is told to complete a task that she cannot do. She begins to worry and cry. At that moment, her shadow mask appears in the form of the tiny dark elf. Her shadow mask in that instance could be named *fear*.

Her fear was of failure—failure to meet another's expectations. The tale insinuates that her shadow mask was one initially given to her by her mother, who taught her how to worry. The mother's worrying was the mask that initiated the trouble of the tale, placing her daughter into a difficult situation. The daughter's first fear was that she wouldn't meet her mother's expectations. She then extended her fears to include the king's expectations and finally the tiny black elf's expectations.

But the story reveals a truth about shadow. It wants to show you the process of assimilating this part of yourself. The young girl held the power to assimilate this dark aspect from the start of the tale, and the dark elf even says so himself. He points to his own undoing—to the magic word with the ability to lift the spell. He says that as long as she does not know his name, she will be his. The converse of his statement could then be true: "When you do know my name, I will be yours." This shadow mask was calling out to the girl, wanting to be brought into the light.[12] In the story, the girl gained control of her fear by looking it in the eye and naming it for what it was. Once she knew the name of the shadow mask, it went shrieking into the darkness from which it came, never to return.

Splitting

How many times have you heard that a focus on negativity will get you nowhere? When I did the work of owning my shadows, I got messages from other people like, "Stop being negative," "You're so gloomy," or "Why are you being moody?" I saw that those who said these things were typically people who disowned the dark aspects of their spirit. These were people who were attempting to split it off from themselves. Now I'll give you a new message: a purposeful focus on negativity will get you everywhere.

The universe yearns for wholeness and unity. Since you are made of the substance of the universe, unity is hard-wired into your body and soul. Just like the universe, your individual spirit yearns for wholeness, and it naturally attempts to reclaim that disowned part of itself.[13] When you purposely deny this unity, you are doing what I call *splitting*.

Splitting is a denial of the existence of your shadow mask, but this denial can have tragic results. What would happen if you broke your arm, but consciously attempted to keep the bones from mending? You would render your arm ineffective. Similarly, you are spiritually crippled when you split with your own shadow masks.

No matter how diligently you try to hide them, they will find ways to reveal themselves. They do so because, just like Tom Tit-Tot, they want to be undone. If you bring your shadows into the light and honor them, you have begun naming, the initial stage of the journey toward assimilation.

The Shadow Mask Exercises

The following sequence of exercises is designed to assist in the naming process of the shadow mask. The techniques are simple: guided imagery and sacred artistry. These will be the keys to finding your shadow masks.

Guided imagery takes you out of the critical mind, the analytical part of us all that judges, analyzes, and edits. Guided imagery is like having a dream that someone else creates for you. The images used in the coming exercises are based on the symbols of myth.

The unconscious speaks in symbols, archetypes, and imagery. It does not comprehend words, but the meanings of words and the meaning behind words are clear to the unconscious. The words of the following guided imagery hold meaning that carries great potency because they are based on the archetypes found in mythology. The words are just the starting point; they propel you into the world of the unconscious.

To get the most out of the exercises, try having the words pre-recorded, or have a friend read them to you. Start by either lying down or finding a comfortable sitting position and closing your eyes. Your body should be relaxed and its movement kept to a minimum.

The next step within our sequence of exercises will be sacred artistry. The images that you see in the meditation will form the basis for your art. Creating art in this way is important to your magical process because its effects are similar to the guided imagery. Art is another non-linear way of exploring your spiritual self. When the sacred artist within you is allowed to run free, you are finding a way to tap into your unconscious, dark material. Once it is brought into conscious light, it can be named.[14]

Shadow Play: the Chamber of Masks

You may have more than one shadow mask, but there is only one that is your *primary* mask. This is the one you will work with for this exercise. Other aspects or masks of your shadow can be named as well, but be sure to work on only one aspect at a time.

Also keep in mind that focused concentration on shadow work for too long a period of time can lead to a psychic imbalance. Remember, just as the moon waxes and wanes, there are times to explore the dark and times to live in the light. If the work of shadow becomes too uncomfortable, take time to do mundane work. When you refocus your consciousness in this way, you will find that you are once again grounded.

Meditation: the Chamber of Masks

Close your eyes and imagine that a soft white glow is forming at your feet. It begins to swirl upward and it forms a protective shell around you. It lifts you up and takes you on a journey to the core of your being.

The misty glow sets you down and dissipates to reveal a marble staircase that spirals downward. The light is very dim along the walls of the staircase and you can't see all the way to the bottom, but you know that this is a place into which you must venture.

You begin down the staircase and you notice that it spirals in a counterclockwise direction. The light in the staircase comes from candles flickering in small carved niches along the walls. The staircase walls are made of smooth, cold marble that you occasionally touch as you continue to journey downward.

As you work your way down the stairs, notice on the walls that there are occasionally sigils, magical symbols formed out of metal and embedded into the stone walls. These are the symbols of your shadow masks. Take note of whichever one is most prominent. This is the symbol for your primary shadow mask.

Reach up and touch the symbol of your primary shadow mask and you'll find that it comes loose from the wall. As you hold it in your hands, you can feel the cold weight of the metal symbol and you can see it from all sides. Hold on to this symbol as you continue down the stairs.

When you reach the bottom, you find before you a great golden door. You try the door, but it is locked. Look at the keyhole and you will find that it is oddly shaped. Slip the metal symbol you hold into the keyhole and you'll find that it unlocks the door. Open the door and enter the chamber.

The room is cold and quite dark, except for a single point of illumination that emanates from the far side of the room. The light comes from a mask that hangs on the far wall. Go over to it and look at it. You notice that it is well within reach, so you take it down and examine it thoroughly. On the inside of the mask is its name. Take note of it.

After you've examined the mask, place it on your face and ask: "How do I resolve this shadow mask?" Listen carefully to the answer.

Once you've heard the message, ask this: "What do I have to learn from this shadow mask?" Once you've received your message, ask one more question: "What does this shadow mask keep me from doing?"

After you've queried the mask, take it off and place it back on the wall. Exit the chamber and lock the door with the metal symbol you retained. As you climb the stairs, you can place the symbol anywhere along the wall and it will set itself within the marble. Continue to head to the top of the stairs, this time moving much more quickly than before.

Once you have reached the top, the white glow enfolds you once again, lifts you up, and brings you back to your body.

When you have arrived back fully, take a moment to contemplate your experience, using the journaling space below.

Journaling

Use the space below to draw the symbol of the primary shadow mask.

Next, use the following space to draw your shadow mask. This will help you in the mask-making exercises to follow.

What is the name of your shadow mask?

What part do you play in keeping this shadow mask alive?

What are the effects of this shadow mask on your life?

What does this shadow mask keep you from accomplishing?

What action must you take in order to resolve your primary shadow mask?

What have you to learn from this shadow mask?

The Elemental Naming of Shadow

All shamanic paths look to nature for spiritual inspiration. The trees, the sun, the moon, the earth herself and all her seasons are a metaphorical framework upon which traditional magical people hang their spiritual philosophy. One clear example of this metaphoric or symbolic thinking is found in what Witches and shamans call the *elements*. Basically, the idea of the elements is that all life as we understand it is composed of four basic qualities: air, fire, water, and earth.

You need air to breathe; fire is your life spark, your energy; your bodies are made mostly of water; and you are solid, made up of earth materials.

These elements are also symbolic. They not only sustain your physical life, but support your spiritual life as well. Air symbolizes your ideas, thoughts, communication, and all beginnings or initiations. Fire symbolizes your passions, your drives, your ability to take outward action, and your ability to *will* or direct energy consciously. Water is the symbol for your emotions. It speaks of your love, sadness, joy, and even your fears, which cycle in and out of your life, rising and abating just like the tides. Spiritually, water symbolizes your powers of intuition and the ability to dare, or muster the courage you need to step beyond the places that are brightly lit or well known. Earth is the symbol for manifestation, solidity, and growth. When you are able to make something happen, or when you build, create, or complete you are working with earth as a symbol, as an energy.

Each of these elements has both light and shadowy attributes. The light attributes emanate from the "deosil" (clockwise) spiral, which focuses your spiritual attention on beneficial self-aspects. The shadowy attributes emanate from the widdershins spiral, which focuses your spiritual attention on detrimental or harmful self-aspects. Below is a listing of some shadowy attributes for each of the elements. Decide which element best suits the energy of your shadow mask.

Air

- ◑ **Direction:** east.

- ◑ **Color:** yellow or clear.

- ◑ **Tools:** wand/staff.

- **Rules:** the mind, mental processes, knowledge, communication.

- **Time:** dawn.

- **Season:** spring.

- **Jewel:** opal.

- **Incense:** frankincense.

- **Animals:** birds and all flying creatures.

- **Aromas:** bergamot, caraway, dill, lemon balm, pine, sweet pea.

- **Shadowy Traits:** forgetful, incommunicative, overly talkative, unintelligent, overly analytical, non-creative, air-headed, blindly optimistic, changeable, fickle, unreliable, restless, inconsistent, two-faced, frivolous, superficial, a gossip, gullible, only able to understand that which appeals to the intellect.

FIRE

- **Direction:** south.

- **Color:** red.

- **Tools:** athame/sword.

- **Rules:** energy, life spark, flames, assertiveness, passion.

- **Time:** midday.

- **Season:** summer.

- **Jewel:** ruby.

- **Incense:** sandalwood, dragon's blood, copal.

- **Animals:** lizards, snakes, dragons, and reptiles of all sorts.

- **Aromas:** basil, bay, juniper, nutmeg, rosemary, rue, woodruff.

- **Shadowy Traits:** angry, furious, rageful, combative, overly aggressive, extreme, overly driven, overly passionate, overly sexed, anxious, tactless, irresponsible, selfish, unsubtle, self-centered, impulsive, quick-tempered, impatient, arrogant, snobbish, intolerant, opinionated, patronizing, power hungry, conceited, exaggerating, only able to relate to that which is extreme.

WATER

◖ **Direction:** west.

◖ **Color:** blue.

◖ **Tools:** cup/cauldron.

◖ **Rules:** feelings, emotions, tides, intuition, the unconscious.

◖ **Time:** dusk.

◖ **Season:** fall.

◖ **Jewel:** aquamarine.

◖ **Incense:** amber, lotus, myrrh.

◖ **Animals:** whales, dolphins, porpoises, fish and most swimming creatures.

◖ **Aromas:** chamomile, gardenia, jasmine, myrrh, rose, lily.

◖ **Shadowy Traits:** overly emotional, weepy, depressed, sad, uncontrollable, lacking energy, non-assertive, indecisive, "weak-willed," too dreamy, easily confused, dishonest, hypersensitive, touchy, moody, self-pitying, unforgiving, jealous, resentful, secretive, overly suspicious, vague, careless, only able to understand emotional content.

EARTH

◖ **Direction:** north.

◖ **Color:** green.

- **Tools:** pentacle.

- **Rules:** the body, growth, material matters, money, stability, structure, death and birth.

- **Time:** midnight.

- **Season:** winter.

- **Jewel:** quartz crystal.

- **Incense:** pine, patchouli.

- **Animals:** four-legged mammals.

- **Aromas:** cypress, patchouli, tulip, vetivert, oak moss.

- **Shadowy Traits:** dense, overly practical, worrier, lacking foresight, controlling, dependent, overly critical, mean, non-spiritual, too grounded, possessive, lazy, self-indulgent, static, inflexible, greedy, stubborn, resentful, overly routine, fussy, hyper-critical, pessimistic, conventional, only able to understand what is perceived through the senses.

Exercise: Mask Making

Making a physical representation of your shadow mask can be liberating. You can feel empowered, because you have better control of the shadow when you can see it before you. Once you externalize the shadow mask, you know what it is made of. You drain it of any power it holds over you because you no longer hide from it. You then gain magical power because you have changed your consciousness and now know when the mask is worn and when it is not.

Below are some methods for making your own shadow masks. Be sure to do the work during the time of the waning or dark moon to maximize the effect of "externalizing" the shadow mask. The waning moon is a symbol for depletion, dissipation, dispelling, or diminishing because the moon appears to "lose" its light. Symbolically, the tide of the waning moon is the time for diminishing or destroying the effects of something. In the case of working with the shadow mask, the waning moon cycle is a magical current that helps to decrease its effects.

MAKING A MASK BASE

Items Needed:

- Mixing bowl
- 1 cup water
- 1 cup flour
- ¼ cup white glue
- 20-30 pieces of newspaper (or paper towels) cut into 1" x 6"strips
- Plastic wrap

DIRECTIONS:

In a mixing bowl, pour 1 cup of water. Add flour in ⅓ cup increments. As you add each ⅓ cup of the flour, stir it well, using your fingers to break up any clots. Once the flour and water are completely combined, it should have the consistency of plaster—thick and muddy. Add ¼ cup of white glue to the mixture and again, stir well with your fingers.

Cut paper into strips. Have your partner lay down in either a sunny spot or lay some towels or newspaper down so excess mixture won't set into the carpet or flooring. As your partner lays down, place the plastic wrap on her or his face.

IMPORTANT: *Create breathing holes in the plastic at the site of your partners nostrils and mouth.*

Dowse paper strips with plaster mixture—one piece at a time. Shake off excess mixture from paper strip and even smooth either side of the strip to take off more of the mixture. The less excess mixture there is on the paper strip, the less time it will take for it to dry on your partner's face.

Begin to lay strips along the outer rim of your partner's face: along the brow, the temples, the jaw and the chin. Be sure to overlap and interconnect all of the paper strips as you lay them out. Smooth each strip into the others with your fingers. Next, lace strips across the nose and connect those strips to those along the rim at the cheek bone area. Once that section is laid, you can begin to fill in the empty spaces on your partner's face around the cheeks and forehead.

IMPORTANT: *Be sure to repeat this entire process a second time to create a stronger mask base.*

Drying time can vary depending on the heat levels at the time of application. To speed this up, try using a hand-held blow-dryer to help "set" the mask.

Once the mask base is dry enough to withstand being taken off your partner's face, set it in a place that gets plenty of warmth. It will take about 24 hours before your mask is fully set and ready to be decorated.

Buying a Mask Base

Many people purchase a "mask base" from an arts and crafts store. A mask base is an all-white face-form usually made out of thin plastic. Occasionally you might find one formed from wood, rag pulp, or plaster. The preferable choices for this exercise are the wood or rag pulp bases because they are biodegradable. This is important because you will need to later destroy the mask in the upcoming purging ceremony.[15]

Mask Decoration

Once you have purchased a mask base, you will want to decorate it so that it closely resembles your internal shadow mask. In some cases, however, this may be a near impossibility. In those cases, instead of working directly from the mask image revealed in the guided imagery, try going to an outdoor setting to gather twigs, pebbles, grasses, leaves, and other natural decorating items that can be incorporated into the mask.

Use the image of the shadow mask found in the mask chamber to guide you in your decoration process. If you would like to add more symbolic value to the mask, try using the elemental listings on the previous pages to help guide your inspiration. Use your imagination and create what seems to resonate most clearly with your shadow mask.

After Completion

When you have completed the shadow mask, set it in a place of prominence. Some people like to create personal altars where they can place sacred objects. The personal altar can be in any room as long as it can go relatively undisturbed. You should be the only one to handle the objects that lay on your altar, for they carry your power.

After the mask is in a place of prominence, spend time each day looking at it. Wonder about it. Ask it questions. Ask yourself questions about it. Live with the shadow mask for some time and become comfortable with the fact that it represents a reality that you once hid. Let that reality be known and accepted consciously before moving into the next chapter.

Notes

1. C. G. Jung, R.F.C. Hull (trans.), Joseph Campbell (ed.), *The Portable Jung*, New York: Viking Press, 1971, p. 145.

2. Jeffrey S. Victor, *The Satanic Panic*, Chicago: Open Court Books, 1993, pp. 202–205.

3. See, e.g., Jeffrey S. Victor, *The Satanic Panic*, Chicago: Open Court Books, 1993.

4. Mario Jacoby, Verena Kast, and Ingrid Riedel, *Witches, Ogres and the Devil's Daughter*, Boston: Shambhala, 1992, p. 24.

5. Jacqueline Small, *Awakening In Time*, New York: Bantam Books, 1991, p. 46.

6. Henri F. Ellenberger, *The Discovery of the Unconscious*, New York: Basic Books, 1970, p. 707.

7. C. G. Jung, R.F.C. Hull (trans.), Joseph Campbell (ed.), *The Portable Jung*, New York: Viking Press, 1971, pp. 146–147.

8. Jacqueline Small, *Awakening In Time*, New York: Bantam Books, 1991, p. 51.

9. This is an archaic term used to mean the past tense of "spin." See, e.g. Jean L. McKechnie (ed.), *Webster's New Universal Unabridged Dictionary*, (2nd ed.), New York: Simon and Schuster, 1979, p. 1737.

10. My retelling is based on the tale "Tom Tit-Tot" retold by Joseph Jacobs, *English Folk and Fairy Tales*, (3rd edition, revised), New York: G. P. Putnam's Sons, (n.d.) pp. 1–9.

11. Jacqueline Small, *Awakening In Time*, New York: Bantam Books, 1991, pp. 51–52.

12. See, for example, how psychoanalyst Verena Kast interprets the tale of "The Black Woman," a similar shadow mask to that found in the tale of Tom Tit-Tot. Verena Kast, "How Fairy Tales Deal With Evil," in M. Jacoby, V. Kast, and I. Riedel, *Witches, Ogres and the Devil's Daughter*, Boston: Shambhala Press, 1992, pp. 27–30.

13. This is a theory promulgated in transpersonal psychology. See, e.g., Jacqueline Small, *Awakening In Time*, New York: Bantam Books, 1991,

pp. 41–45; see, e.g., John Wellwood (ed.), "Befriending Emotion," in *Awakening the Heart*, Boston: Shambhala Press, 1985, pp. 79–90.

14. See, e.g., Gabriele Lusser Rico, *Writing the Natural Way*, New York: J.P. Tarcher, Inc., 1983, pp. 96–97.

15. However, if only plastic mask bases are available, use them and alter the purging ceremony so that you do not leave plastic out in a natural setting.

Chapter 3

SHADOW AS THRESHOLD GUARDIAN

The Sage speaks:

The effort required to hold back darkness is wasted effort. It would require a greater power than any known in the Universe to hold darkness in check, for it is an aspect of the whole great cosmos! Try to stop the sun from setting. You will always wind up in the dark. When you resist it, you embrace it unwittingly.

And know this: you must have all your wits about you when facing the great darkness of your own spirit. Do not fool yourself into believing the child's tales told by simpletons, "There is nothing in the dark that isn't already in the light." Going into your darkness unprepared and unarmed is not worth doing. The task of making the assay through the darker labyrinths of spirit is wondrous and miraculous—a journey of healing, not a frightful thing. Once you begin this journey in fear, you have begun with a constricted heart, and it is your heart that is needed, for it is privy to a great body of knowledge.

The dark will ask many questions of your heart, but know that where there are questions, there must also be answers.

Beyond the presence of the shadow is the unknown, the threatening void, and shadow uses the threat of this to its advantage. It keeps us in patterns of behavior that are comfortable and well known, which are the ways of "the community,"[1] as Joseph Campbell puts it. The ways of the community take us down paths that are brightly lit, but that ultimately go nowhere for the one who wishes completion and power. It is not the issues of the community that are the primary focus of the magical work of the Witch or shaman. Once caught by the community, you can find it difficult to move beyond it, even if its ways are not in your best interest.

Living solely within the compound of the village, constantly repeating familiar patterns, is not where the power of the Witch, shaman, or mystic lies. The community stands for human order. The shamans and Witches of tribal cultures move beyond the order superimposed by others out of spiritual necessity, in order that their journey toward power should go uninhibited.

That is not to say that no order at all is a preferable way of exisiting within a community. But a shaman is one who consciously explores the boundaries imposed by others and often crosses over those limits to bring back new information. The difference between a shaman and a "madman" is that a shaman can come back from a journey beyond the cultural limits and can resume a functional role within the community. A shaman or Witch is flexible and moves "between the worlds" of man-made order and cosmic order. A "madman" also explores the limits of what is acceptable by the culture, but does not do so consciously, nor can she or he return from beyond at will.

In every fairy tale and myth throughout the world, the heroine or hero begins as a member of the "community," but then ventures into the world of the unknown, beyond the limits. As these tales begin, characters commonly operate within the strictures, codes, and laws of the village or kingdom. This symbolizes the idea that they operate mostly within the mundane world, created by a society that often operates with indifference to matters of spirit. That is when trouble usually arrives—the golden ball gets lost, the princesses disappear every night, or the cow runs dry and must be sold for beans.

Once trouble appears on the horizon, it is time for the heroine or hero to face a period of transition, for passing through a threshold. The threshold is a boundary space between what is known and what is not. The difficulty or trouble that propels the tale's adventurer into encounters with unknown forces is a manifestation of the shadow.[2]

Of course, all of the symbols found in the tales of the fairies apply to us, and this encounter represents the second phase of working with the shadow mask. When we dare to move beyond the confines of the known and approach the unknown—a threshold—we will always find our shadow guarding the gates to whatever lies beyond, to whatever power we might claim just beyond the village gates. The shadow is the keeper at the gate that detains us. It presents to us the riddles of the sphinx; it tells us that beyond its bounds lies the unanswerable. It whispers in our ears all of the doubts and worries that can plague us throughout our lives. The shadow, in this aspect, makes us question ourselves. Though this prospect may seem a bit daunting, it is this aspect of your shadow that begins the process of making you whole, of weaving together your light and dark qualities.

Here then is a tale of a questioning shadow—a threshold guardian.

Che Red Eccin

Long before time, there were two brothers who lived with their mother in a faraway land. One day, it came time for the eldest son to make his way in the world. Before he left his home, he gave his brother a magic knife and told him that as long as the blade stayed shiny, he would know that his brother was safe, but if the blade became rusty, then he would know that his brother was in trouble. The younger brother accepted this gift with gratitude.

So the eldest bid his mother farewell and set off into the countryside. Before long, he came upon an old shepherd. The roving youth asked to whom the sheep belonged. The shepherd told him that they belonged to a fierce beast named the Red Ettin of Ireland. This shepherd also told him to beware of the beasts of the field he should next meet.

So the young man went on and soon he came upon a multitude of dreadful beasts with two heads and four horns on each head. He was quite frightened and waited in hiding for a chance to run away as fast as he could. He was glad when he was able to run at top speed away from the beasts. He soon came upon a castle that stood on a small hillock. He approached the castle and found an old wife sitting outside. He asked her if he might stay the night, as he was weary from travel. She said that he

might, but that this was the castle of the Red Ettin, a terrible beast with three heads who spared no man's life. The young man would have gone away, but he was afraid of the beasts outside the castle, so he asked the old woman to hide him as best she could and not to tell the Ettin he was there.

Soon enough, the Ettin came home and noticed the scent of an intruder in his castle. He began to tear apart the rooms of the castle until he finally found the young man. He pulled him out of his hiding place and said: "If you can answer me three questions, your life will be spared." So the first head asked, "What is a thing without an end?" But the young man did not know. Then the second head asked, "The smaller the more dangerous, what's that?" But the young man could not answer. Finally the third head asked, "What is dead, yet carries the living?" But again, the young man knew not an answer. So the Ettin took a mallet, struck the youth on the head and turned him into a pillar of stone.

Back home, the younger brother noticed the magical knife that his elder brother had given him had become brown with rust. He knew his brother was in trouble. So the younger brother bid his mother farewell and set out into the countryside in search of his brother.

On his way, he came across an old woman who asked if he could share a piece of his bread with her. He shared what little he had, and lo and behold, she transformed herself into a radiant being. The transformed woman told the youth that she was a fairy, and in return for his kindness she would give him a magic wand that would be of service if he were to use it for good. Then the fairy told him a great deal of what would happen to him in his near future, and what he ought to do in all circumstances. After that, she vanished from sight.

Soon the boy continued on his journey. Just as his brother had, he came upon the old shepherd, who told him that the sheep he tended belonged to a terrible monster called the Red Ettin of Ireland. Soon the youth was continuing on the path again, just as did his brother, and he too saw the beasts just outside the castle of the Red Ettin. But he did not stop nor did he run away, but went boldly through amongst them.

Soon the youth came to the castle, knocked on the door, and was admitted. The old wife inside tried to warn him of the Red Ettin, and of the fate that had befallen his brother, but he demanded admittance to the castle.

The monster soon came in and siezed the young boy. Once again, the Ettin said, "If you can answer me three questions, your life will be spared." He was given the three questions, but because the young man had been told everything by the good fairy, he was able to answer all the questions. So when the first head of the Ettin asked, "What's the thing without an end?" he said, "A bowl." And when the second head said, "The smaller, the more dangerous, what's that?" he answered, "A bridge." And when the third head asked, "When does the dead carry the living?" he youth replied, "When a ship sails on the sea with men inside her." When the Ettin heard this, he knew his power was gone. The young man then took an axe and hewed off the monster's three heads.

The boy then found his brother who had been turned into a pillar of stone. He touched the fairy's magic wand to him and his brother started back to life. He also took the great treasure of the Ettin, and when all was in his possession, he and his brother went home to live happily from then on.[3]

Application of "The Red Ettin"

The story of the Red Ettin depicts an encounter with shadow as a threshold guardian, which is similar to the role of an initiator. *Initiation* is a word used in spiritual paths to denote a transition point during one's spiritual journey. This transition point usually involves a symbolic death and rebirth, just as crossing a threshold involves leaving one sphere and entering another.

In the tale, the shadow poses three questions or riddles that seem unanswerable. This symbol tells us that shadow does indeed test us. Your shadow mask—your behavior—will similarly ask questions of you in an attempt to keep up the illusion that there is nothing beyond it. It wants you to think that you cannot live without it. It wants to stump you so that you will continue to cooperate with it, so that you are in its power. It keeps you behind the gates that open to whatever it is that lies beyond cultural limits. It does not want you to move beyond the limits of your previous realm, beyond your previous behaviors and ways of being in the world. Most shadow masks have so much power over us that it inevitably feels painful to cut back their influences.

This theme of the shadow as a threshold guardian—one who initiates you into power—is a common one throughout the world's mythologies and fairy and folk tales. For instance, tribal folk of Central Africa describe an apparition called the Chiruwi. If he is ever encountered along the plains, the Chiruwi challenges the journeyer to fight, says the tale. If the journeyer wins the fight, the apparition will plead: "Do not kill me. I will show you lots of medicines." Then the journeyer becomes a person of power. But if the Chiruwi wins, his victim dies.[4] Thus the shadow presents us with only two options: become its slave, which is symbolized as physical "demise" in the folklore surrounding the Chiruwi, or meet the shadow's challenge and become transformed.

The tale of the Red Ettin clearly reiterates this idea of the two paths you can take once the shadow calls you to initiation. Having no answer, in essence claiming no power in the face of the shadow, is the first path. In the tale of the Red Ettin, this is the path of the elder brother. The Ettin asked his three questions, and the brother failed to answer. The result of this path is paralysis, the inability to move in effectual ways through your life. In other words, you are enslaved by the shadow. The brother who became a pillar of stone was the symbol of this principle. When you have no answer for the shadow, when you cannot meet the challenge of initiation, you too fall under the spell of the Red Ettin, and your consciousness becomes as inflexible as a pillar of stone.

The second path, which is illustrated by the younger brother in the story, is that of meeting the initiation of the guardian shadow by having answers. But how can we have the answers? They are given to us at the hands of what the story calls a "fairy."

But what exactly is this "fairy" from the tale who prepares us for the assay? To best understand the symbolic value of the fairy, we need to look once again at the study of symbols, dreams, and myth, which all emanate from the same zone of the psyche—the unconscious.[5] Dream analysts and Jungian folklorists suggest that one way to read a dream or fairy tale is to consider each element of the story as part of the dreamer or reader.[6] From this perspective, you could say that the two boys of the fairy tale are aspects of yourself. But if this is true, then both the Ettin and the fairy woman are part of your consciousness as well. The fairy woman is an aspect that you can access in the face of the shadow, which is your own personal Ettin. The fairy aspect is your innate wisdom. The fairy symbolically represents your light consciousness, your beneficial, affirmative, constructive affect, and your inherent wisdom.[7] The questions asked by the shadow may feel unanswerable, but in truth they are questions to which you already know the answers. The unconscious houses both your light and dark qualities, and you have access to both at any time throughout your life's journey. You need to bring forth wisdom from your light self to answer the questions of the dark self in order to move through the shadowy threshold of initiation.

Once properly prepared at the hands of the character represented as the "fairy" of the story, the younger brother was able to pass the tests of the shadow (in this case, the Ettin) and take its power over him away. The key to passing the initiation of the shadow is access to your inner wisdom.

There is one other aspect of the shadow initiator you need to know before you begin the journey of preparation: the shadow has a self-giving aspect. Although the task of passing through the shadow's doorway may seem unattainable, it is important to know that your way is never completely blocked. It presents to you its test to reveal to you its weakness, which represents the entry point through which you can pass. What this means in practical terms is that once you can face the call of the shadow by providing answers to its supposedly "unanswerable" questions, you rob the shadow of its power over you. What's more, by giving you a test, your shadow shows you that it can be won; it offers itself to you in this roundabout way. By revealing its weakness, it is telling you how to master it.

This self-giving aspect of the shadow is one that is made manifest in some initiation rites throughout the world. For example, in the arduous initiation rites of the Arunta tribes in the Australian outback, the youths preparing for the initiation are held captive for long periods of time, during which they are fed on the blood of their initiators.[8] This blood-eating ritual is common among the various tribes of the Aborigines, and it serves to illustrate the idea that the shadow can actually be a source of spiritual nourishment, if you are able to assimilate its presence through initiation.

The initiation rites of certain Wiccan traditions illustrate another such manifestation of the principle of shadow or initiator as a nurturer.[9] In several traditions, there is a ceremony called "the passing of power." At a certain time in the growth of a Wiccan initiate, when the initiate is ready to face greater responsibility and become an elder, an initiator wills all of his or her power to the initiate.[10] Thus, at the hands of the initiator, the initiate's spirit is fed, and similar to the young Aboriginal initiates, a Wiccan priestess or priest passes from the innocence of youth to the wisdom that comes with maturity.

The Ettin, initiator, or shadow does not want to consume you as much as it wants to heal you, to nurture you. The tale of the Red Ettin provides a clue to help you face the shadow's nurturing initiation. When the second youth comes across wisdom, symbolized by the old beggar/fairy woman in the tale, he is able to answer the call to initiation. It is the fairy who tells the youth how to answer the Ettin's initiating questions with success so he can pass through the threshold that allows him his "reward" in the conclusion. It is this same aspect of your consciousness that will guide you through the shadow initiation.

Exercise: Embracing Wisdom

This exercise entails meeting the inner Crone or Sage, which is the personification of your wisdom. In this exercise, men may discover either a Crone or Sage as the personification of their inner wisdom. Women may tap into either the female or male archetype dwelling within as well. To say that men can only connect with the inner Sage and women only their inner Crone would be magically untrue. Exclusion through specific gender assignment of roles takes the Witch or a shaman away from the diversity of consciousness needed not only to be creative, but to make magic.

Undeniably, men will never have the full gender experience of being female, nor may women ever fully understand what it is to be male, but opening ourselves to imagination is one way of deepening understanding and empathy,[11] as well as broadening the scope of our magical power. There is no sense in resisting the form, whether male or female, that your wisdom wishes to take. Try to remain open to the possibilities of this exercise.

A Word on the Symbolism Used

In this exercise you will be taking a classic shamanic journey to connect with your higher consciousness. Some call this force the higher self, the spirit guide, the wisdom self, or even the guardian angel, depending on the spiritual tradition.

Most shamans and Witches have at least one spirit guide that personifies this wisdom self. However, the idea of a spirit guide is not exclusive to those shamans who claim lineage to Northern and Western Europe; the figure is common to shamanic and magical people globally.[12] For example, according to the anthropological literature regarding the shamans of Siberia, shamans have a spirit guide which they call a "tutelary spirit." Thousands of miles away in Mexico and Guatemala, the shamans communicate with a spirit guide called the "nagual."[13] In the Polynesian magical tradition called Huna, shamans call the wisdom self the "Amakua."[14]

Whatever the name, contact with the wisdom self is essential to magical work—especially work that concerns the shadow. It is this portion of your consciousness that you will be contacting during the upcoming meditation.

Also, within the meditation you will use an astral or spiritual form of what was historically called "the Witches' flying ointment." Witches and magical flight are two images that are inextricably intertwined. Although this concept may seem fanciful, it is one that has actual historic roots. Fairy tales, and later on, mass media forms popularized this lore surrounding the magical flights of Witches.

In sorting out the realities from fantasies, the important factor is the flying ointment itself, which was according to all accounts a noxious combination of poisonous and hallucinogenic herbs blended into a salve and applied to various parts of the body. The reports surrounding the use of ointments made frequent mention of flight, journeys to other worlds, and transformations into animals and other creatures.

Although you will not be using a physical ointment, you will use an astral one to symbolically unlock your higher spiritual potential. The two forms of ointment produce the same effect, but the spiritual form will not create the side effects that the ancient Witches endured (usually prolonged illness and then death).

Finally, in the exercise, you will be using the glyphs or signs of both the moon and sun:

The sigil of the moon is one of the signs of women's power and wisdom; the sun is traditionally associated with men's power and wisdom.

It may be useful to have a partner read the instructions for the following meditation exercises out loud, or else record them and play them back while meditating.

Meditation: The Keeper of Wisdom

Close your eyes and take several slow, deep breaths. With each breath sense where in your body you hold tension and allow it drain into the ground, into the earth, where it is neutralized.

Imagine that a blue mist begins to swirl around your feet in a counterclockwise fashion. The mist slowly begins to climb your body. It covers your ankles... now your knees... now it covers your pelvis and your waist... now it covers your middle body and your chest, hands, and arms... now it covers your head and envelops you completely, like a cocoon.

The mist begins to lift you and take you away from the room to a sacred place that your spirit will recognize. It is journeying to a place that it has been before. It is taking you back to the place called the shadow chamber, where your mask resides. The journey is long, but you are traveling at speeds beyond sound or light or time.

[**Partner: pause for ten to twenty seconds of silence.**]

The mist begins to set you down now and to dissipate. As it does, you find yourself at the top of a staircase that spirals downward to the shadow chamber. Go down the stairs. As you spiral downward, look along the wall for the magical symbol that opens the door. This symbol will be embedded in the marble walls, but will detach from the wall as you touch it. Take the symbol and go to the bottom of the spiral staircase, where you will find the door to the chamber. Unlock the door and move into the room.

There on the far wall is your shadow mask. Go over to it and take it from the wall. Since this is your second time in this room, your eyes seem to be more accustomed to the dim light and you can see features you couldn't see before. In the adjoining wall there is a fireplace, with an old heather broom leaning close by. There is a small table near the fireplace, too. On the table is a jar with ancient designs inscribed on it.

This jar contains the sacred ointment of the priests and priestesses. It is the ointment of sacred visions. Open the lid of the jar, take a dab of the ointment on your fingers, and rub it into your third eye, which rests in the middle of your brow, at a point between your eyes.

When you do this, notice that your body becomes lighter, almost weightless. Your feet barely touch the floor and your arms are like feathers. Hold on to the mask and stand before the opening in the fireplace. Before you know it, you are pulled up into the dark recesses of the chimney. Feel your body rush skyward through the chimney. Soon you are out of the tunnel-like space of the chimney and you are flying through the night sky with your mask.

[**Partner: pause for a moment.**]

Soon you are gradually set down on the mist-covered ground. The time is midnight, and you find yourself on a dirt path that travels through a gully between two close, wooded hills. As you walk along this path, you look into the night sky and see the waning moon. It is a thin, pale yellow crescent in the heavens.

As you journey along this path, you see a small cottage or hut just ahead. A flickering of light emanates from what appears to be a window or some other opening in the side of the structure. Approach this cottage. Go to the doorway, knock on the door, and wait to be admitted.

The door opens silently by itself to reveal an elderly person sitting by a fire. This wizened one beckons to you.

Ask this wise one's name.

[**Partner: pause for a few seconds.**]

Show this wise one your mask and ask what questions this mask will ask of you. Ask what you will need to know in order to confront this mask and pass its initiation.

[**Partner: pause for two minutes.**]

If you do not understand how these answers apply to your shadow, ask now.

[**Partner: pause for one minute.**]

After you have received your answers, this wise one will hand you a magical tool that you can use to transform the darkness. What is this tool, and what are the powers associated with it?

Thank the wise one when you are finished, and let the blue mist begins to swirl once again around your feet. It begins to cover your body once more. When indeed you are covered, you begin to lift up. You are brought back to the place where your body rests comfortably, the place that exists in ordinary time and space. Journey now back to your body. When you are back in your body, the effects of the flying ointment will have disappeared completely. When you are ready, open your eyes and answer the journaling questions.

JOURNALING

What is the name of the wise one you encountered?

What are the questions this mask will have for you?

What are the answers you need to know in order to face the shadow effectively?

What was the tool given to you and what are its powers?

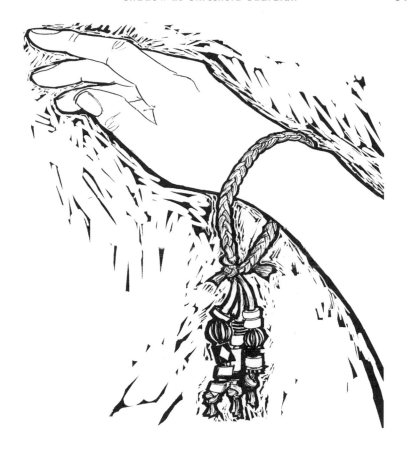

The Shadow Bracelet

The shadow bracelet halts the effects of the shadow mask in your life. This is the first step in transforming the effects of subshadow from a downward pull on the psyche to a true internal power. Once you know when the shadow mask appears in your life, you have a better chance of working with it for growth. For now, it is best to halt the negative effects of the shadow mask, which is what the shadow bracelet helps you to do. However, this tool is not meant to establish a full resolution or assimilation of shadow.

It is easy to make and to use, and it is highly effective. The idea behind the shadow bracelet is to become consciously aware of each behavior generated by your subshadows. Typically, shadow mask behaviors are destructive or in some way harmful to yourself or to others, which makes them easy to detect. Shadowy behaviors influence your feelings of empowerment (or non-empowerment) and can indirectly affect how others view you and consequently how they act toward you. Halting the effects of the shadow mask can have immediate and transformative effects.

Whenever a shadowy behavior arises while using the shadow bracelet, stop for a moment and ask yourself how this behavior is related to subshadow, to stuffed away emotions.

Constructing the Shadow Bracelet

Items needed:

- ◖ String or yarn. Be sure to use colors that are connected with your shadow mask's colors.
- ◖ Beads. The beads should have mouths wide enough for threading the yarn or string. Again, you should use beads that correspond to the energies of your shadow mask.

Measure the yarn or string using your arm. Take the tip of the string and hold it between your first two fingers. Measure out enough to go down the arm to your elbow.

Now measure out two additional lengths of string of the same length. Tie the three lengths together in a knot, leaving five inches off the end, to form a bit of a tassel. Using the longer portion of the remaining yarn/string, begin to braid them all the way down until only two inches remain.

Tie the ends together, so that the braid does not come undone. Cut off two of these three remaining ends. Use the last end to tie a knot just above the first knot at the top of the braid; this creates the bracelet's loop. You will be tying the loose end onto the tassel end. You should tie the knot loose enough so that you can widen the bracelet to fit you comfortably.

String up the beads on each of the three ends of the tassel and knot off the ends of the string/yarn so that the beads cannot come off.

Using the Bracelet

Whenever you recognize a shadow mask behavior, flip your wrist from side to side, until the beads begin to slap up against your arm and rattle together. Take a moment to reflect on the possible origins of this mask. After that, say the following mantra, which is a prayer to either the Crone or the Sage Goddesses and Gods:

> I call to thee in the triple sign
> (Mother/Father) darksome and divine,
> Bear with thee the holy sword,
> To cut the darkness with a word.

Notes

1. Joseph Campbell, *Transformations of Myth through Time*, New York: Harper & Row, 1990, p. 37.

2. Joseph Campbell, *The Hero With A Thousand Faces*, New Jersey: Princeton University Press, 1973, pp. 51–52.

3. Retold by the author from retelling of "The Red Ettin," by Joseph Jacobs, *English Folk and Fairy Tales*, (3rd edition, revised), New York: G. P. Putnam's Sons, (n.d.) pp. 136–142.

4. David Clement Scott, *A Cyclopaedic Dictionary of the Mang'anja Language Spoken in British Central Africa*, Edinburgh, 1892, p. 97.

5. C. G. Jung, Joseph Campbell (ed.), "Dream Symbolism in Relation to Alchemy," *The Portable Jung*, New York: Viking Press, 1971, pp. 324–325.

6. C. G. Jung, Joseph Campbell (ed.) "Dream Symbolism in Relation to Alchemy," *The Portable Jung*, New York: Viking Press, 1971, pp. 324–328.

7. It is a core belief in traditional psychoanalysis that the personality and the unconscious warehouse both light and dark qualities. In order to have full access to our light qualities, however, we must embrace and assimilate the dark. See, e.g., Jacqueline Small, *Awakening in Time*, New York: Bantam Books, 1991, p. 41.

8. R. and C. Berndt, "A Preliminary Report of Field Work in the Ooldea Region, Western South Australia," *Oceania,* XII (1942), p. 323.

9. Primarily these initiation rites are those of the English Traditional Witches. Gardnerian, Silver Crescent, Alexandrian, Kingstone, and Georgian traditional initiations are especially illustrative of this aspect of the self-giving initiator.

10. This rite is found in the Gardnerian second degree initiation. See, e.g., Morven Forest (ed.), *The Rites as Practiced by Ouroborous et Ova,* "Second Degree Elevation," Chicago: Gardnerian Rite Church.

11. William Kurtines, Jacob Gewirtz, *Moral Development Through Social Interaction,* New York: John Wiley & Sons, 1989, pp. 103–110.

12. Ruth F. Benedict, "The Concept of the Guardian Spirit in North America," *Memoirs of the American Anthropological Association,* Menasha, Wisconsin, 1923, v. 29, 67.

13. Michael Harner, *The Way of the Shaman,* New York: Bantam Books, 1986, p. 54.

14. Brad Steiger, *Kahuna Magic,* Gloucester, MA: Para Research, 1971, p. 19.

Chapter 4

ASSIMILATION

The Sage speaks:

I can see that you are held back. I know what troubles you, my child, for I have known the spirit with which you now wrestle. This spirit's name is Past. Past determines what your limits will be, and so Past is truly the guardian of the magic, the guardian of power you can ultimately attain.

The realm of Past is not easy territory to traverse. It is laden with bramble and thorn of old pain that threaten to reopen wounds, but it is also lush with trees filled with the ripened fruit of past happiness. Past wants us near. It draws us close so that those brambles may be cleared. The wounds from Past threaten to kill you, but they inevitably heal.

This journey is a good omen, but heed this warning, my child: if you dare to venture into Past's realm, tarry not long there. Go to Past only for its healing and return without delay. For Past's pathways are brightly lit but go nowhere—only in circles. Paths that lead to desired destinations are direct, but can many times be darkened, mired paths. Which path is finally in your best interests? Why, you know the answer and have always known.

Wise ones know that Past carries a secret fear of their power to move into the future, which ultimately controls Past's influence. Remember that Past is stupid and cannot create anew. It has no vision, only hindsight. Past may have the power to define where you came from and who you are, but it cannot say who you will be! Look into the future, my dearest, set your sights somewhere in its swirling unformed mists, and the spirit of Past becomes inactive. It knows it has lost you when you side with the future.

Tell me, my beloved, what does Past whisper in your ear right now?

CHILDE ROWLAND[1]

Once there were four children—three boys and one girl—who were all born into the royal family of a distant kingdom. One day, when they were still young but on their way to maturity, they stood outside on a moss-covered knoll and played together with a golden ball. The eldest child, Burd Ellen, kicked the ball with such force that it went over the top of a nearby holy mound and down the other side.

Without thinking, Burd Ellen dashed around the side of the mound to fetch the ball, but she did so going widdershins, or counterclockwise. The three boys waited and waited, but Burd Ellen never returned with the ball. She had vanished. They searched for her, but it was all in vain. Poor Burd Ellen was gone.

So, the boys went to the wizard Merlin and asked him if he could say where she was. Merlin thought a moment and then replied, "The fair Burd Ellen has been carried away by the fairies because she went widdershins around the mound, which is the opposite way to the sun. She is now in the Dark Tower of the King of Elfland."

The eldest of Burd Ellen's brothers vowed that he would bring her back from the Elf King or die in the attempt. So he begged the wizard Merlin to tell him what he might do to bring her back. Merlin taught him what he should know, and then the eldest brother set out for Elfland. The others waited long, but the eldest never returned. So the middle brother begged Merlin to tell him what he might do to bring back the others. Merlin taught the youth, who then set out for Elfland. The youngest waited long, but the others never returned.

So the youngest, named Childe Rowland, asked Merlin what he might do to bring back the others. The Merlin said, "Two things: one which you must do and the other which you must not do. Whoever speaks to you in Elfland, you must cut off their heads with a sword. The second thing is that you must not eat anything while you are there in that dark land."

So Childe Rowland, with the Merlin's wisdom in mind and a sword at his side, set off for Elfland. He journeyed for many days until finally he saw someone who was tending fairy sheep. (He knew that they were otherworldly by the fire in their eyes.) He asked the shepherd if he knew the whereabouts of the elf king's Dark Tower. The shepherd did not know, but told the youth to go down the road farther until he met a henwife and that she might know the vicinity of the tower. So without delay, Childe Rowland took out his sword and severed the shepherd's head with one blow.

He came to the henwife some distance from the sheep and asked her the same question. She told him that the Dark Tower was still further on, but in order to get in he must circle round the tower three times going widdershins and chanting: "Open, door! Open, door! And let me come in!" Then he could gain entrance to the Dark Tower. Childe Rowland then proceeded to sever the head of the henwife.

Childe Rowland then journeyed on a bit further until he came upon the Dark Tower. He did as he was instructed; the gates opened, and he entered the Tower. Once inside, he expected the Tower to be as black as pitch inside as was its exterior, but instead it glowed with a soft radiance. The light came from a gigantic pearl that hung in the main chamber.

When he entered this chamber, he was met by Burd Ellen who said, "Why have you come for me? It is no use. You will end up dead like your brothers, who lie yonder."

Childe Rowland did not care to discuss the matter. Instead he told his sister he was hungry and asked for some food. Because she was under the spell of the King of Elfland, his sister could not refuse him the food, though she knew it would be his downfall. She could not warn him, but she looked sadly to the floor and shook her head as she fetched a meal. But Childe

Rowland remembered what Merlin had said and dashed the food to the ground when it came.

In an instant, the doors to the chamber flung open and in rushed the hideous Elf King. Childe Rowland rushed to meet the creature with his sword. Then they fought and fought, till Childe Rowland beat the King of Elfland to his knees, causing him to beg for mercy. Seeing no good in destroying the Elf King, Childe Rowland granted him mercy on the condition that he raise his brothers to life and release them all from his spells. "I agree," said the Elf King, who took out a phial of blood-red elixir. He anointed the two brothers at the five senses, on their ears, eyelids, nostrils, lips, and fingertips, and they soon sprang to life. They told Childe Rowland that their souls had been lost, but were now restored.

Once all had been mended, the four siblings went through the dark halls, out of the Dark Tower, never to return.[2]

Working with the Subshadow

To this point in the journey along the road of darkness you have only worked with the shadow mask. That work centered around resolving your dark and sometimes pernicious behaviors—your outward-directed shadow. You learned that once the shadow mask was recognized and confronted, it would be difficult to wear that mask without conscious awareness ever again. That journey set limits to the shadow mask's influence in your life. For that reason, resolution of shadow at the mask level can mark the end of a journey into personal darkness for some readers.

For others, exploration of the shadow mask only raises more questions. "Where did my shadow mask come from?" "Can I effect the life of a shadow?" The answers to these questions are found in magical work centered around the second layer of shadow called the subshadow. The journey into subshadow culminates in a mystical process called assimilation, which is a method of bringing the subshadow into a form that can be easily taken in or absorbed in the consciousness. However, in this procedure the only parts of the subshadow that are assimilated are those that stimulate growth and a change of consciousness. The magic of assimilation begins with a spiritual odyssey into the past, where the roots of the shadow mask lie.

In focusing on the subshadow, it is fundamental to consider the past's influence on the present shadow mask. Women's experiences with sexism provide an illustration of how the shadow mask (which is like an outward, visible symptom) emerges from the subshadow (which is like the cause of that symptom; it is much like subtext, the meaning behind the words on a page or the history behind the present moment).

When a woman experiences her first brush with blatant sexism, that instance could be characterized as a degrading, disempowering situation. The instance of sexism itself is a shadow mask, a symptom, an affect that comes out of an entire history of women's disempowerment—the subshadow. The feminist movement is the catalyst facilitating a change in consciousness regarding those historical, underlying issues of gender bias. As you will see, the feminist movement is like magical assimilation, because it provides a forum for women to strive toward empowerment on their own terms.

Common sense tells you that where you are, what you are, what you believe, what you know, and how you feel in the present are all directly related to the past—good, bad, or neutral. This by no means implies that the past railroads you into predetermined behaviors. There are always choices for present behavior. No one is absolved from responsibility for the decisions they make regarding their actions. However, what fuels behaviors linked to the shadow mask are past events that typically caused physical, mental, or spiritual pain.

My understanding of the subshadow's origin is that from time to time you are unable to fully absorb certain painful events of your life into your consciousness. Because you don't fully absorb these events, they become like nodes of energy that get trapped in the body, mind, and spirit. Over time, these unassimilated events can lessen your magical potential, rob you of your spontaneity, and cause you to feel weighted down and wounded on all levels.

But what causes the subshadow to form? It is a manifestation of natural human limitations. It is physically impossible to consume an entire meal, digest it, and absorb its nutrients instantaneously. It is just as impossible to accomplish the same task with life's experiences. Each encounter goes through processes similar to physical ingestion, digestion, and absorption. First you take in the details of an event, then you attempt to make sense of it, and finally you endeavor to learn from it. Painful events are especially difficult to absorb in this way. Magical assimilation begins a cycle of healing by breaking apart the trapped energy nodes throughout your interconnected planes of being.

Magical assimilation synthesizes a myriad of approaches because the subshadow permeates your being on distinct, yet integrated planes or levels: physical, mental, and spiritual. An ancient hermetic saying is, "as above—so below," which means whatever happens in the spiritual realm is mirrored in the physical and vice versa. This implies that every plane of existence is interconnected with the next, and when one of these is effected, so are the others. If you work with shadow on the physical or mental planes, then you can effect change on the spiritual. It is clear that a multi-planed magical approach to the subshadow can facilitate assimilation on all levels. An exploration of ideas related to assimilation of the subshadow in psyche, body, and spirit is therefore in order to begin the magical wheels of assimilation turning.

The Mental Plane

In relation to our definition of the subshadow, there are two main theories that link it to the mental plane. One reaches back in time to the emergence of psychology as a fledgling field of study in the Western world. The other is more contemporary, but the two have overlapping features.

Some of the first theories to explore the idea of subshadow claimed that energies of painful past events get stuck inside of us, never losing their original impact. These models of psyche stressed that assimilation happened slowly over time. Freud, Jung, Adler, and even contemporary psychoanalysts theorized that the original events are continuously reenacted in a symbolic way in an effort to resolve themselves.[3] Though these early theories had tremendous impact on understanding subshadow, they proved not to be the final word. They did pave the way for some compelling contemporary models.

One contemporary model that seems to closely match the three-planed, interwoven definition of subshadow is related to behavioral theories of psychology. According to Dr. Francine Shapiro of the Mental Research Institute in Palo Alto, California, unassimilated events of the past become like knots or crystallized energy that get locked into the nervous system.[4] These knots are like barnacles on the hull of a ship that can cause permanent damage or, in some cases, sink the whole boat if not scraped off. She developed a technique called eye movement desensitization and reorganization (EMDR), which breaks up these energy crystals so that they can be more readily assimilated. The theory Dr. Shapiro put forth relates well to several body-centered ideas that work with subshadow.

In magical assimilation, you will experience guided imagery exercises that will tap into this plane of the mind and that will begin to dislodge the energy nodes of the past.

The Physical Plane

The link between the planes of mind and body (or mental and physical planes) is well documented, and it is almost conventional wisdom that whatever you think eventually affects your body.[5] This happens because the nervous system, which is actually an extension of the brain, is the regulation mechanism that tells the body how to operate. The body houses almost 800 muscles. These muscles all have "sensory cells" that link the muscle system to the nervous system, which facilitates communication between the mind and the body.[6] Most of the time we are not conscious of the link between body and mind. There are other times—for instance, during a stress headache—when you become aware of the effects of the link.

According to alternative, holistic health care professionals who focus on mind-body coordination, emotional energy is linked to the muscle mass.[7] They believe that long-term emotional stresses, such as those that evolve from the subshadow, contribute to the tightening of various muscle groups.[8] The specific muscles that tense up under stress differ from person to person, situation to situation. However, over a long period of time, the stored tension weakens the body structure, breaks the natural flow of bio-energy, or natural body energy, and eventually this contributes to the formation of disease. Techniques such as massage therapy, Rolfing, Judith Aston's "Patterning," chiropractic care, and Feldenkrais's work assist in the release of these muscle-linked emotions.[9]

Through the journey of assimilation, you will discover the specific muscle groups that are linked to your subshadow. Work on this plane will ultimately include the use of touch and massage, which can either be done alone or with a magical partner. Before you incorporate a partner into this magical work, be certain to assess your comfort level with the partner's touch.

This work on the physical plane will assist in the release of emotional tension or subshadow energy stored in the body. Now let us turn to the realm of spirit.

The Spiritual Plane

For Witches, shamans, and others with an animistic world view, the term *spirit* refers to the life force that flows through all creation. This force is called *prana* in Hindu theosophy, *mana* in Polynesian shamanism, and *chi* by the Taoists.[10] In each of these philosophies, the realm of spirit is invisible, yet supportive of the physical plane. The physical and spiritual, in turn, connect to the mental plane. The source of life-force energy is the divine, the Universe, or as the Witches say, the Goddess and the God, and a constant and unimpeded flow of that energy facilitates life, health, and wholeness.

According to the Chinese Tao, a balance of life force, chi, generates health and happiness; an imbalance causes disease. In this philosophy, there is no difference in the physical and spiritual planes. They are merely different manifestations of the same energy.[11] So when chi (the spiritual plane) is impeded by the blocked emotions of the subshadow (the mental plane), that in turn can cause excessive muscle tightening in the physical plane, which makes an individual susceptible to illness. Working to facilitate the flow of spiritual energy can effect change on the physical and mental planes.

Each culture approaches its exploration of the spirit plane differently. In the Western mystical tradition—specifically, in Witchcraft—ceremony and ritual are ways to tap into the realm of spirit.

I see ritual as an intentional, symbolic act or set of actions that convey spiritual principles and that are intended to change consciousness. Rituals are often tied to myths, which are themselves elaborate symbol systems. In fact, one definition of ritual is, "the enactment of a myth."[12] Rituals are intended to effect the mental plane through their spiritual symbolism. Symbols address the mental plane and speak to the deepest part of our consciousness—the unconscious. In Western psychology, we know that the unconscious is not a verbal entity. It speaks with the body and uses unstructured sounds, gestures, pains, and bodily expressions to communicate. The unconscious understands the world through our bodies as well; it uses the five senses to give and receive information. It speaks through the symbols of dream, through music, color, and through gestures and other movements of the body.[13]

An important component of ritual in many cultures is the physical plane. This is exemplified through rituals that make use of the body, movement, and dance.[14] Movement facilitates a visceral connection with the unconscious. Through dance and other body movements, the contents of the unconscious are made manifest. For that reason, magical assimilation includes ritualized movement, and through ritual and dance you will simultaneously access the planes of spirit, mind, and body.

Application of "Childe Rowland"

The tale of Childe Rowland clearly marks out the challenge of the subshadow and the healing power of assimilation. In this tale, the subshadow was called the "King of Elfland" and the hero who bravely dared to face this entity was Childe Rowland.

By the time Childe Rowland had journeyed into the realm of the subshadow, he saw the results of the subshadow. It had made his brothers "dead" and had placed his sister under a "spell." This tale is unique in its ability to allow the reader identification with both the hero on his journey and the other characters of the tale who are in peril; we all could be placed under the spell of the Elf King, the subshadow, if we never attempt to find resolution. Once under the Elf King's spell, we are no longer self-empowered. We are shadow-driven which makes us like Childe Rowland's brothers—dead in spirit.

As you recall, the origin of the shadow mask is an unassimilated emotional event. Many times the reason why an event goes unassimilated is that it is threatening, just as the King of Elfland appeared to Childe Rowland. However initially threatening the Elf King may have been in the tale, the end of this story revealed an astonishing quality of this subshadow: it carried the ability to heal, to restore to life what it had killed. This, too, is a quality of your subshadow.

In the tale of Childe Rowland, the wise old Merlin offers us some sound advice: when we are in the land of our subshadow, we must stay firm against the threatening pain of the past. Merlin tells Childe Rowland not to listen to anyone nor to eat anything while in the domain of the subshadow. He said that it would be better to "cut off the head" of past pain than to listen to (or actually, absorb) the pain of the past. He warns Childe Rowland not to eat anything while there either. This bit of advice relates to the idea of not listening to the shadows. If we eat of the shadow, we consume or take in its qualities. To feed ourselves on our past pain brings about our spiritual death, as it did to Childe Rowland's brothers.

Magical assimilation is not a technique to help you absorb the pain you have left unexperienced. Instead, it is a magical way of turning the unassimilated pain around, so that, like the King of Elfland, it has the ability to heal. The promise of this tale is that you too can bring the King of Elfland to his knees and have him restore you to life with his phial of blood red elixir. The journey begins with magical assimilation.

Magical Assimilation

Magical assimilation will involve several steps that specifically address each of the three interconnecting planes of existence. Meditation in the form of guided imagery addresses the mental plane. Massage and body movement work on the physical plane, and ritual touches the plane of spirit.

Each ritual in Wicca, and the rituals you will learn in this book, begin with the creation of "sacred space," which is space set aside for spiritual endeavors. For the purposes of assimilation, you create sacred space by "casting" a dark moon circle. The magic circle symbolizes spirit, as the circle is a geometric shape that suggests an eternal quality that the spirit carries—it has no beginning and no end. Casting a circle delineates the space that will contain the magical, transformative energies you generate during your rituals. The steps for creating a dark moon circle are in Appendix A in the back of the book.

Your journey of assimilation will be in the form of two rituals that take place over two consecutive nights. The first ritual is best done on the last night of dark moon during whatever month you choose. This is the time also known as the fourth quarter of the lunar phases. On the mundane level, there is only one night where the moon is fully dark. In mystical traditions like Wicca, three nights of lunar darkness are observed. Witches observe three nights as a symbol of the three phases of the Goddess—the maiden, mother, and crone. The second assimilation ritual should be done on the night immediately following, which is the time of the first waxing moon, also known as the first quarter. The timing of these rituals symbolizes the end of one way of being in the world and the beginning of a new way: the dark moon signals an ending, and the return of lunar light a beginning.

Be sure to read through each ceremony and guided imagery exercise before attempting your magical assimilation. Once you feel safe doing these exercises, find a partner to read the meditations for you during the rituals, or try reading them into a tape recorder so that you can play them back at your convenience. The magical work given below is used to facilitate this endeavor. Keep in mind that even though you may participate in these rituals, the real work of assimilation is a very slow, daily, internal process. For some people, assimilation is a life-long endeavor. Be patient with yourself and be sure to honor your limits as you go through each exercise.

NIGHT 1: NIGHT OF SHADOWS

darkmoon circle

Moon Phase: 4th quarter, last night of dark moon.

Purpose: to assimilate the subshadow and shadow mask.

Items Needed:

- ◗ Banishing incense.[15]
- ◗ Banishing oil.[16]
- ◗ A red candle.
- ◗ A bowl of water.
- ◗ A dish of salt.
- ◗ Your shadow mask.
- ◗ A pair of scissors.
- ◗ A cauldron, small pot, or other vessel in which you can burn things safely.

The first night's ritual has two distinct sections. The first part includes a guided imagery exercise; the second part is more ceremonial and includes movement, chanting, and dancing. Feel free to pause between the two sections of the ritual to rest, or even discuss your experiences with your magical partner.

On the night when the moon is darkest (the last night in her twenty-eight-day cycle), gather the supplies for this ceremony and find a secluded, peaceful setting for the ritual. It can be done either indoors or outside. Set up an altar in the spot that will be the middle of your magic circle.

Cast a dark moon circle.[17]

Once your circle is cast, find a comfortable spot, lay on the floor, and begin the following guided imagery exercise.

Assimilating the Subshadow

Close your eyes. Begin to scan your body for tension. Begin at your feet and slowly move your consciousness upward through your body. Where are you holding tension? Wherever that is, take a deep breath and as you exhale, breathe through the tension and allow it to melt away from your body, into the ground where it is neutralized.

After you feel relaxed completely, take another deep breath and imagine that a blue mist is beginning to swirl at your feet in a counterclockwise direction. The mist covers your body completely, and when it does, it lifts you and takes you back to the shadow mask chamber.

When the mist sets you down, you are at the top of a spiraling staircase that leads downward. Follow the stairs until you see your special metal symbol, inlaid within the marble walls. This symbol represents your shadow mask. Take that symbol from the wall and continue to spiral downward until you reach the doorway to the chamber.

Unlock the door with the metal symbol and enter the chamber. You will see your primary shadow mask illuminated on the far wall. Go over to it, take it down, and place it on your face.

As soon as you do this, you find yourself speeding through a tunnel of time. Colors and faint images pass on all sides of you, and soon you are transported to a scene from your past. This is the moment in the past when your subshadow was created. Allow this scene to play before your spirit eyes. Notice what age you are in the scene. Notice the people involved in the scene.

[Partner: pause for at least two minutes.]

Now allow yourself to feel the emotions that this scene is evoking. Bring these feelings into full conscious awareness. As these emotions come forward, take note of where you feel them in your body. If you have a partner, tell this person now where you feel the emotions. If you do not have a partner, take a mental note of where the emotional energy is held.

[Partner: wherever in the body the emotions are felt, place your hands on that spot and carefully, gently begin to massage that area.]

Wherever in your body that feeling is being held, breathe into it, make it bigger and bigger with each out-going breath. Continue to watch the scene in front of your spirit eyes and allow yourself to feel the enlarged emotion. Sustain this feeling with your breath for as long as is possible and allow yourself to physically let out your feelings as you watch the scene—cry, moan, yell—do whatever your body needs for you to do to dislodge the pain that was once stuck inside of you. Do this while you continue to lay on the ground with your physical eyes closed.

[Partner: pause for at least five full minutes, or until the meditator has completed her or his catharsis.]

Special note: *It may take the meditator several minutes to open up to her or his emotional states. Continue to encourage the meditator to express the emotional state. If there is no catharsis, discontinue the meditation and try again in 28 days, during the dark moon phase.*

Allow this feeling to subside now. Let it soften.

[Partner: again allow a couple of minutes for the charged emotional state to subside and soften. You may end the massage work at this time.]

Now imagine that you lift up and float above the scene you've been watching. Feel how you are becoming lighter, easier, more tender and tranquil as you rise up out of the scene. You are taking the vantage point of the higher self—the wisdom self, where you are beyond the extremes of human emotion. Imagine that you actually become your higher, wisdom self.

From this vantage point above the scene, watch all the players involved in the scene and, magically, the meaning of this scene will become clear. There was a lesson to learn—what was it?

er you come to an understanding of the scene, begin to take breaths. Notice that with each deep breath, the shadow mask ιre wearing feels as though it is shifting and becoming warmer, lighter, brighter. The colors of the mask change, and the shape changes, too. You cannot see it fully yet, but you can sense the changes occurring. The mask has become light; it is assimilating more fully into your consciousness. It now has a new name, a name of strength. It has now become an ally of yours. Listen within, and the new name of strength will be clear to you.

When the mask has stopped changing form, continue to breathe deeply and slowly, and notice that as you do, the scene from the past fades away. Continue breathing deeply until the scene is completely gone and you find yourself back in the dim recesses of the shadow chamber. When you are fully within the chamber, take off the changed mask and look at it. What has it become now? Observe the colors, shapes, designs, and other decorations it has now assumed. Look inside the mask and there you will see printed the name that this power has become. What strength is this mask lending to you?

Once you know this, it is time to leave the shadow chamber. Climb the stairs once more and return the symbol to the wall (if it has not disappeared or changed as well). If the symbol has changed, notice what the symbol is now.

At the top of the spiral staircase the blue mist begins to wrap and swirl around your body. Once it completely covers you, it lifts you up and takes you back to the place where your physical body rests comfortably.

Once you are fully back, open your eyes, stretch, and take time to answer the journaling questions either aloud to your partner or in written form in the space provided below.

If you do not have a magical partner, locate the place in your body that held the subshadow energy and gently massage it for several minutes to facilitate subshadow movement on the physical level.

JOURNALING

What is the new name of the mask?

What power does this changed mask lend you?

What action is needed on your part to retain this power?

Draw here the new mask: (You will use this in the ceremonial portion of the ritual that will follow.)

Purging Ceremony

Hold in your hands the shadow mask you made in earlier exercises. Starting in the west, and continuing counterclockwise, present it at each of the four compass directions: west, south, east and north. At each compass point, hold the mask up high and say:

> Guardians of the (west, south, east, north),
> Behold the power of the night!
> Shadows that once danced now take flight!

Next, chant the name of the shadow mask over and over until you feel psychic energy beginning to build within you. If the chanting is not enough to generate psychic energy, try dancing around the circle in a counterclockwise direction. Allow the chanting to grow louder until you reach a climax point. That is the point at which you will have created a vortex of psychic power, or as the Witches say, a "cone of power."

At that point, use your scissors to cut the shadow mask in half. To heighten this moment, try screaming or extending a long sigh. During this, imagine that some of the energy vortex is used. After that, cut those two halves of the mask into halves, so that there are four pieces.

Hold your hands over the quartered mask and direct the rest of the energy vortex into the mask pieces. As you direct this energy, visualize the subshadow leaving through your hands and imagine that it becomes confined to the mask pieces.

Take one piece of the mask along with your cauldron or other vessel to the western quarter. Light a match and burn the mask piece in the vessel. While it smolders, extend your arms so that the palms of your hands are directed towards the west and say:

> Shadow, bound and restrained
> Mirror of self—my non-self.
> I bind thee and I return thee,
> To the darkest void
> Of the outer spaces!

Repeat this process at each of the remaining three compass points with your other mask pieces. Be sure to move around the circle in a counterclockwise fashion: west, south, east and then north. When you have finished this, scoop together the ashes of the mask and set them aside for later.

Next, sprinkle yourself with the water and salt mixture you used to cast the dark moon circle. With this, dab a bit on to each of your five senses: apply it to your hands, your ears, on your brow between your eyes, and on your lips. Repeat this process with the smoldering banishing incense to symbolize a cleansing with air and fire. Hold your hands over the smoke and then use your hands to fan the incense on to your ears, eyelids, nose, and mouth.

Finally, anoint yourself with banishing oil in the same way on each of the five senses to represent their awakening to life.

Close the circle.

After you have closed the circle, take the ashes from your burned shadow mask and dispose of them ceremonially by scattering the ashes to the four winds. Take the ashes to the ocean, a lake, or stream and scatter them in the water, or cast the ashes into a hole you dig in the ground and cover them over.

While you discard the ashes, you may chant the following or even create your own magical chant:

Triumphe supra umbra!
Sins incurrere pleores!

Translation from the Latin:

I conquer my shadow!
Protect me mighty ones from its danger!

The deed is done. Subshadow has been ceremonially banished. This concludes the first night's ritual.

Night II: First Light

Moon Phase: 1st quarter (first night).

Purpose: To assimilate the positive qualities of the transformed mask.

Items Needed:

- A red candle.
- A dish of salt.
- A bowl of water.
- Incense of your choice.[18]
- Mask-making supplies.

On the first night of the waxing moon cycle, gather your supplies and cast a circle, but this time, cast a standard circle instead of a Dark Moon one.[19]

Within your circle, purify the mask-making supplies by passing each through all of the elements. Sprinkle a bit of water and salt on them, pass them through the candle flame (if that is safe and possible), and pass them through the twisting smoke of the lit incense.

After the mask supplies have been purified, begin to assemble them, creating the new mask you saw in the meditation of "Night I: Night of Shadows." This new mask is called the "Mask of First Light."

Once it is complete, place it on your altar at the center of the circle. Begin to dance deosil—sunwise—while chanting the name of the new mask. For instance: "Radiance...radiance...ra...di..ance...." As you dance, start out slowly, chanting the name softly. As the dance progresses, begin to make it wilder, louder, and full of your magical intent, which is to assimilate these new qualities. There are no dance steps to this magical movement that are more important than the ones you create. Spontaneity is the key. Try not to allow your critical mind to interfere with this process of creativity. Don't edit whatever may come up in your magical movement. There are no incorrect movements in this dance. This dance encourages the process of becoming. It is a technique that allows us to leave the negatives of the past behind. In the process, the future, new qualities come into being.[20]

As you dance, imagine that you gather magical energy and form it into a cone of power or energy vortex. Listen to your intuition and when it tells you that you have gathered enough magical energy for the transformation and assimilation, stop the dance. Extend your hands over the new mask. Draw on the energy you have created and imagine that you are sending the energy into the new mask. While doing so, chant:

> I assimilate the virtues
> Of the mask of first light.
> In me, through me, by me, be me!

When you are finished, sit comfortably and place the mask on your face. Ask yourself internally, "What will be the first visible signs in my life that this mask has transformed me?" Wait for the answer. Then ask, "What are the first actions I must take to keep this mask alive?" Listen to the voice of your inner wisdom and when you have the answer, take that action when you can.

Celebrate the new assimilation with cakes and wine, the traditional Wiccan celebratory meal. When all is done, close the circle.

Notes

1. This tale is actually a cante-fable, which is a mixture of folk tale and verse. The cante-fable is a very ancient form of the English fairy tales and harkens back to a time when stories were told or performed, rather than written. It is speculated that the verse parts of the cante-fable might have been sung in such a performance. Joseph Jacobs, *English Folk and Fairy Tales*, (3rd edition, revised), New York: G. P. Putnam's Sons, (n.d.), p. vii.

2. Joseph Jacobs, *English Folk and Fairy Tales*, (3rd edition, revised), New York: G. P. Putnam's Sons, (n.d.), pp. 122–129.

3. Henri Ellenberger, *The Discovery of the Unconscious*, New York: Basic Books, 1970, pp. 480–500.

4. Francine Shapiro, *Eye Movement Desensitization and Reprocessing Workshop Manual*, Palo Alto: Francine Shapiro, 1989, p. 2.

5. See, e.g., Ron Kurtz and Hector Prestera, M.D., *The Body Reveals*, New York: Harper & Row, 1984.

6. Thomas Hannah, *Somatics*, New York: Addison-Wesley Publishing Company, 1988, pp. 13–14.

7. See, e.g., Ron Kurtz and Hector Prestera, M.D., *The Body Reveals*, New York: Harper & Row, 1984, pp. 6–11.

8. See, e.g., Thomas Hannah, *Somatics*, New York: Addison-Wesley Publishing Company, 1988.

9. Ron Kurtz and Hector Prestera, M.D., *The Body Reveals*, New York: Harper & Row, 1984, p. 11.

10. See, e.g., David E. Bresler, Ph.D., "Chinese Medicine and Holistic Health," in Arthur C. Hastings, Ph.D., James Fadiman, Ph.D., and James S. Gordon, M.D., *Health for the Whole Person*, Boulder, CO: Westview Press, 1980, pp. 407–419.

11. David E. Bresler, Ph.D., "Chinese Medicine and Holistic Health," in Arthur C. Hastings, Ph.D., James Fadiman, Ph.D., and James S. Gordon, M.D., *Health for the Whole Person*, Boulder, CO: Westview Press, 1980, pp. 407–419.

12. Betty Sue Flowers, (ed.), Joseph Campbell, *The Power of Myth*, New York: Doubleday, 1988, p. 82.

13. See, e.g., Loretta Malandro, Larry Barker, and Deborah Barker, *Nonverbal Communication*, New York: Random House, 1983, pp. 94–117.

14. See, e.g., Denny Sargent, *Global Ritualism*, St. Paul: Llewellyn Publications, 1994, p. 55.

15. See Appendix B for recipe.

16. See Appendix B for recipe.

17. See instructions in Appendix A.

18. I recommend using White Moon Incense. The recipe is in Appendix B. However, any incense that seems to stir your unconscious processes is helpful.

19. See Appendix A for the standard, deosil circle-casting format.

20. Paul Davies, *The Mind of God*, New York: Touchstone, 1992, p. 34.

Part II

Spirals:
Dark Moon Power

...And thou who thinkest to seek me, know that thy seeking and yearning shall avail thee not unless thou knowest the mystery: that if that which thou seekest thou findest not within thee, thou wilt never find it without thee. For behold, I have been with thee from the beginning and I am that which is attained at the end of desire.

—from *The Charge of the Goddess*

Chapter 5

The Widdershins Spiral

The Sage speaks:

In the ways of magic, balance is all. It is from balance you are born; this is the balance of the earth, your Mother. Her life force, Her equilibrium reverberates within all, and through it She maintains all in Her mystical earthly web.

Remember that a fruitful tree cannot bear fruit when the season turns. The tree must have a time of rest and rejuvenation. For during that time when its leaves wither on the bough, its movement is mostly internal. This tree is actually gaining in strength so that in the spring it can blossom and fruit once more. So go the ways of magic.

The life of magic ebbs and flows just as surely as the light of the moon. There are times of movement and there are times of rest. Just as the fruit tree's magic bursts forth from its times of internal movement, so must yours. Honor these tides of your power and your magic will be strong, for you shall live within the ordanes of the Great Ones.

ᴄHE WIDDERSHINS DANCE

Widdershins means counterclockwise; in Neopagan parlance, it specifically means to go against the direction of the sun. Within the sacred circles of Witches and shamans, the word *widdershins* describes the movement of energy that is "reverse" to that of sunwise or "deosil" energy, which is active and focused toward outward manifestation. Widdershins energy is rarely used within the Witch's circles; in fact, most practitioners' only exposure to this work is annually at the great festival of the Celtic new year, Samhain.

At that time, spiritual communities called covens celebrate the passage through the dark gates of the Lord of Death, which is one of the many aspects of the Celtic Horned God, Cernunnos. Death is a natural part of life for pagans, Witches, and shamans, who believe that the entire universe and all her creatures are a manifestation of deity, of spirit. Witches believe that deity is the source of life energy and this energy swirls into physical form. It takes the shape of humans, plants, animals, stars, and planets. This energy can swirl out of physical form as well. Humans experience this at the time of death. Neopagan spiritual systems celebrate death not in its aspect of ending, but as a transition point from one state to another. At Samhain, Witches dance widdershins around the magic circle in honor of this reverse cycle, which moves spiritual energy out of physical form.

The circular widdershins dances hold power and many more layers of meaning beyond that which is currently observed in traditional Wicca. For instance, anyone who has studied meditation knows that death is not the only time that spirit spirals out of form, away from its physical manifestation. Meditation is a way of providing brief periods that are similar to that of a dormant fruit tree, when it seasonally ceases to bear fruit. The tree is not dead in these periods. Its action becomes internal while it refuels from its source, its spirit, the earth.

Similarly, the waning and dark moons are symbols for the work of consciously focusing our attention inward to draw power from spirit. The dark moon is a symbol for these periods of internal magic.

Clearly, a tradition that honors the power of an inner craft is missing from contemporary Wicca. But how could such an important element be missing from the contemporary Craft? The fact that there are gaps in the existing practices of Witches is understandable, since the Craft is reconstructed from the myths, lore, and customs of the tribal Europeans, a people whose mostly oral traditions of religion and magic were forced underground (and many of them lost) with the invasions of the Romans and Christians. Because of this, contemporary Witchcraft is a constantly evolving discipline.

With this in mind, I began to explore ideas that might help reconstruct the missing inner tradition of contemporary Witchcraft. What resulted from my search was a new vision of the Witch's power that included a cycle of reverse energy that I call the *widdershins spiral.*

DARK SPIRALS

At the time of the waxing moon and at many of the Eight Great Sabbats, Wiccan celebrants utilize a dynamic technique to generate psychic power through circular and sometimes spiraling dances. Through the dance around the circle, past the four elements (air, fire, water, earth) represented at each of the compass points (east, south, west, north), Witches create a swirling cone of power, the essence of magic that they use to create outward action, movement, or change.

This outward-directed power must be fueled from some source. For Witches, the source is deity—the Goddess and God—who suffuse their very bodies, minds, and spirits. Access to the Gods and their powers occur when Witches shift their locus of consciousness from the external to the internal world.

The moon both waxes and wanes, which illustrates that magic occurs in cycles, pulsations of both external and internal movement. You need both cycles to achieve a natural balance in your personal, spiritual power. The widdershins spiral is the power cycle that coils you back to the center of your being, to touch the sacred source of Witch power, and arouse inward movement and illumination.

If there was a sacred, spiraling dance created for widdershins magic, it would move past the same four deosil elements of the magic circle. But instead of starting in the east, in the element of air, the widdershins spiral would begin in the west, in water. It would swirl past fire, then air, and then earth, and return to water in the west.

The energies of the widdershins spiral are like the twin brothers and sisters of air, fire, water, and earth. They are born from the same four elements, and as many brothers and sisters do, they create tension. Widdershins powers create an opposite or reverse polarity to that of their brother and sister energies in the deosil spiral. This polar tension is the source behind all movement in magic.

Working in both directions—deosil and widdershins—is the balanced path of the Witch and shaman. Another way of describing the two paths is to say you can either work magic from the outside to the inside or from the inside to the outside, depending on the moon's cycle. The waxing moon symbolizes magic that starts on the outside; the waning moon is symbolic of magic that starts within.

If, for example, you light a green candle every day to create some sort of change, this would be working magic from the outside to the inside. You light the candle in order to create magic, which is a change in consciousness. You do not have to concentrate on creating consciousness changes because the physical candle becomes a psychic trigger, setting the internal powers of the unconscious in motion.

If you begin magical work from the point of the unconscious—for example, by meditating on the purpose of lighting the green candle— you are working magic from the inside to the outside. By meditating on the purpose, you do not necessarily need the green candle because you begin with a shift in consciousness. However, mediation that does not translate into action is useless.

Thoughtlessly lighting a green candle is ineffective. But in combination, their magic is potent. You need both cycles, internal and external, to walk the path of the Witch and shaman in balance and power.

The double spiraling design found throughout Europe serves to illustrate the relationship and the interplay between these two ways of working magic.

The double spiral design has been found primarily in European archaeological sites that date back almost 8,300 years.[1] This mystical symbol emerged as a pottery design in the second half of the seventh millennium B.C.E. in Thesaly. It later spread throughout Old Europe and was a common design from 5500 to 3500 B.C.E.[2] The design seemed to be a favorite among the Celts; it was often incorporated into their jewelry and pottery designs and appeared on the walls and facings of long barrows.[3] The double spiral design serves as a symbol of regeneration, of the cyclical, reciprocal power exchange between polar energies such as life and death,[4] positive and negative, active and passive power.

This interplay between polar energies—called the "spiral dance"[5] by pagans and Witches—is the dance of the eternal spiraling of our lives: birth, growth, decay, death, and rebirth. Incarnation moves steadily toward excarnation; excarnation moves us into the next incarnation, and the round never ends.

The sunwise part of the double spiral, which starts from a center point and moves outward in consecutive rings, is the first half of the double spiral. It serves to symbolize the stage through which spiritual energy manifests in a physical form. It also symbolizes the time when you work magic from the outside to the inside—when you use the physical world to make change in the internal, in your consciousness.

The counterclockwise or second part of the spiral, which starts from the outer rings and recedes toward the center, symbolizes the stage in which energy moves out of (or even away from) its physical form, such as through meditation. In a meditative state, you move your consciousness away from physical action toward spiritual action. For Witches, meditation is the time of working magic from the inside to the outside. It is using the internal world to make change in the physical.

WIDDERSHINS ENERGIES

Whether accessing power in a deosil or widdershins way, the path of the double spiral treads past the four compass directions and lends us power from each of the elements. East, south, west and north represent the elements air, fire, water, and earth respectively. Let us look at both of these power cycles to clearly note differences in meaning of the elements and compass directions when they become widdershins powers.

DEOSIL QUARTERS

When we generate magical power through the deosil spiral, the east is the place of beginnings, and it imparts the power *to know*. Knowledge, insight, and communication are key powers evoked in the east. The south is the place of growth, passion, and the life spark. It teaches us the power *to will*. The place of endings, of decline, is in the west, which brings forth the power *to dare*. The west's power brings forth our emotions, such as courage, joy, anger, and sadness. The power *to be silent* belongs to the north, which is the place of wisdom, death, and mystery.

Deosil Elements

In the deosil spiral, the alchemical elements represent human qualities and characteristics. Air is representative of knowledge, communication, and birth, while fire symbolizes our drive, ambition, and aggressive impulses. Water symbolizes the tides, ebbs and flows of our lives, and is closely aligned with women's mysteries and our emotions. Earth symbolizes materialization, stability, and fertility.

Generating Deosil Power

The deosil energy spiral starts in the east, the place of beginnings where you initially gain knowledge (east, air). Once that knowledge is assimilated into your consciousness, your consciousness is then raised and you acquire wisdom (north, earth). Once you are wise, you then can feel the courage (west, water) to take action (south, fire), which then leads to physical manifestation.

Widdershins Quarters and Elements

When the spiral of energy moves widdershins, taking you within, each of the quarters and elements becomes a point of tension, pulling in the opposite direction to that of the deosil spiral. This psychic tension is a necessity in the generation of magical energy. Each of these new widdershins powers are stages of consciousness you experience on the journey within toward a meditative state. But they are also psychological attitudes that can be powerful and transformative. They are accessible to you at any time with a little practice.

The widdershins spiral begins in the west, moves to the south, to the east, to the north, and then circles to the west once more. The tension point of water—the west's power to dare—becomes the power to accept in the widdershins paradigm. In order to dare, to go beyond the limits, beyond the known, you should know what the limits are. The power to accept is that which grounds you in the here and now, so that you can see the reality of both your limits and assets.

In the south, the tension point for fire, the power to will is the power to surrender in the widdershins spiral. Most people find it difficult to associate this term with power. However, in our new power structure, surrendering has many layers of meaning. It means the ability to relax the body and mind, to let go so that you can tap the source of power behind willing, which is spirit. It also means "to allow the processes of nature to unfold." Both of these types of surrendering are advantageous, especially when on the way to apprehending internal power, as you will see in the upcoming chapters.

The tension point for the east, air, which is the power to know becomes the power to wonder. Knowledge begins with wondering. The power to wonder opens your mind to roaming beyond the limitations of knowledge into the zone of unlimited creativity and spontaneity. When you operate from knowledge, you are the teacher; when you wonder, you are the student. Witches, shamans, and all manner of mystics aim for flexibility of consciousness, so they assume both roles.

In the north, the tension point for earth, the power to be silent becomes the power to resonate in widdershins magic. Resonance is the doorway through which wisdom, direction, and divine power enter your life. It is the point at which the Goddess and God fully enter your consciousness and your entire being. It is a form of divine possession through which you resonate with and then assume their powers. The deosil term *to be silent* means to create a void. The void is filled when you claim your power through the Goddess and God by resonating with them.

Direction:	Deosil:	Widdershins:
east	to know	to wonder
south	to will	to surrender
west	to dare	to accept
north	to be silent	to resonate

Element:	Deosil:	Widdershins:
air	knowledge, communication	wondering, moving beyond what is known
fire	passion, tension	relaxation, release
water	emotions, intuition	grounding, presence
earth	manifestation, material goods	inner-manifestation, spirituality

Generating Widdershins Power

In combination, these polar powers of the widdershins spiral spin you in the direction of inner growth, movement, and manifestation. You begin this movement by accepting where you are in time and space and honoring your limitations and attributes honestly (west, water). Once you have done this, you have surrendered (south, fire) to reality; then you begin to relax mentally and physically. Once you surrender in body and mind, you open your consciousness up to wondering beyond the bounds and limitations of knowledge (east, air). Once you have opened your consciousness to wonder, you slowly begin to resonate with the Universe (north, earth). You then operate from the perspective of the big picture, or the macrocosm, because you have melded with the Goddess and the God.

Beginning the Work

In each of the chapters that follow, you will once again find fairy tales as your guides through the world of widdershins power. Each chapter also includes exercises, meditations, and rituals to help you access these dark powers within. Take each lesson at your own pace, for these powers are potent and transformative. They expand your consciousness so that growth can occur. Once you shift your axis of power and the locus of your magical control to "within," change is inevitable.

The Sage speaks:

> *From west to north go 'round and soon,*
> *Resonance will be the boon.*
> *Spiral in, then back to west,*
> *Thou hast begun the sacred quest.*

Notes

1. Marija Gimbutas, *The Language of the Goddess*, San Francisco: Harper-Collins, 1989, pp. 279 291.

2. Marija Gimbutas, *The Language of the Goddess,* San Francisco: Harper-Collins, 1989, p. 279.

3. Just a few of the many striking archaeological remains with the spiraling motif include Maiden Castle hillfort in Dorset, England (c. 300 B.C.E.), The Turoe Stone in County Galaway, Ireland (c. first century B.C.E.), and the walls and surrounding stones at Newgrange tomb in Newgrange, Ireland (c. 3200 B.C.E.). See, e.g., Maria Gimbutas, *The Language of the Goddess*, San Francisco: Harper-Collins, 1989, and David Bellingham, *An Introduction to Celtic Mythology*, New Jersey: Chartwell Books, 1990.

4. Marija Gimbutas, *The Language of the Goddess*, New York: Harper-Collins Publishers, 1989, p. 204.

5. See, e.g., Starhawk, *The Spiral Dance*. San Francisco: Harper-Collins, 1989.

Chapter 6

The Power to Accept

The Sage speaks:

The first task of the magical apprentice is to open the eyes. Ah, my wise one, look deeply into my mirror. What is it that you see? Look deeply my child, and a vision of reality will come clear. However painful, however joyful the vision, stay within its limits for the moment. Though you could easily set aside the unbiased mirror and conjure images of life as you want it to be, or even imagine things as they once were, it is best to know that these are illusions. Once time stands still, you live within the moment and are at the center of all power. Look into my mirror, my beloved, and see things as they are now—for magic changes the inner workings of the heart, mind, and spirit—and we cannot change until we know what it is that needs changing!

The Goose Girl

Once there was a princess who was betrothed to a prince that lived in a far away kingdom. The princess' good mother prepared the girl for her journey. She gave her plenty of gold and silver, as well as many other jewels and treasures befitting a young woman who was about to be a royal bride. And she also gave the princess a waiting maid to ride with her and give her into the bridegroom's hands.

Both the waiting maid and the princess were given horses, but the princess' was a gift from a kindly fairy who had loved and guided the princess since birth. The fairy's horse was an enchanted beast named Falada, who had the power of speech.

When the time came for them to set out, the fairy said to the princess, "Take care of Falada, dear little princess, for she may be of use to you along your journey." The princess took in the kindly fairy's words. Then she got upon the horse and set off on her journey to meet her bridegroom.

As they were riding along, a good distance from the princess' home, the young girl asked the waiting maid to use the golden cup and fetch her some water from a nearby stream. The impudent maid refused her, saying, "If you are thirsty, go get the water yourself! I shall not be your waiting maid anymore!"

The princess got down off the horse and knelt over the little brook and drank. She was frightened and dared not bring out her golden cup. She cried and said, "What shall become of me?"

The enchanted horse called to the princess in hushed tones, saying, "Princess, if your mother only knew, this day she would rue!" The princess was very gentle and meek, so she said nothing about her maid's ill behavior, but got back up on the horse and continued the journey.

As they rode on, the day became so hot that the princess asked once more for the maid to fetch her some water from a nearby stream. The maid replied more rudely than before, "Fetch the water yourself, wench, I'm no longer your maid!"

The princess got down off the horse, and leaned down to drink at the little brook. As she drank, she cried, saying, "What will become of me?"

The horse once again replied, "Princess, if your mother only knew, this day she would rue!"

When the princess was done drinking, she stood up and found the maid now astride Falada. The maid said, "I shall ride Falada, you may have my horse in exchange." Not only this, but soon the princess was forced to take off her royal clothes and put on her maid's ragged ones. The unfaithful servant threatened to kill the mistress should she ever tell anyone what had happened. But Falada saw all that had happened and remembered it.

Once they came upon the royal court, they were met by great revelry and joy. The prince met the two women, lifted the false bride into his arms, thinking this was his bride to be, and took her upstairs to the royal chamber. The true princess was instructed to stay in the courtyard below.

Now, the old king spied the lovely princess in the courtyard and inquired about her. But the treacherous false bride told him, "That is a servant I brought to wait on me. Please give her something to do so that she will not be idle." So the old king had the princess sent to help a lad who took care of the geese.

Then the false bride said to the prince, "Do me this one favor: have the horse I rode in upon slaughtered, for it was unruly and troubled me along my way." But the truth was that she was very much afraid that Falada would one day tell the truth of what she had done to the princess. The prince fulfilled her wish and had the beast killed.

When the princess heard of it, she cried and begged the slaughterer to nail up Falada's head against the large dark gate of the city, so that she might see her sometimes. The slaughterer took pity on the poor girl and did as the princess asked.

The next morning, the princess, now known as the goose girl, went to work with the goose herder. The geese made their nests just outside the walls of the city, so they had to pass through the dark gate. At the gate she mournfully sighed, "Falada, my poor horse! What shall become of me?"

To which the head answered, "Poor little princess, you should be the bride. If your mother only knew, this day she would rue!"

This happened the very next day as well. As the princess and the goose herder went through the dark gate on their way to work, she mournfully sighed, "Falada, my poor horse! What shall become of me?"

The horse's head would always reply, "Poor little princess, you should be the bride. If your mother only knew, this day she would rue!"

This so disturbed the goose herder that he went to the old king and said, "I cannot have that strange girl helping me with the geese any longer. She talks to a dead horse's head at the dark gate and is sullen all day."

"Tell me more," replied the king. The goose herder told the whole story of what happened every day at the gate. The old king told the boy to go out with the goose girl one more time, and when morning came, the king placed himself behind the dark gate. He heard for himself how she called to Falada and how she answered her.

The old king went home without being seen and when the goose girl came back in the evening, he asked her why she spoke so to the horse's head. The princess burst out into tears and said that she must not tell anyone or she would surely lose her life. But the old king begged her so hard that she would have no peace until she told him the story word for word.

It was very lucky for her that she did so, because the king ordered royal clothes to be put upon her at once. So transformed was she that she was quite dazzling to the eyes. And so radiant was she that she was beyond recognition. The king told his son that his was a false bride, a waiting maid, while the real bride, the princess, stood by. The prince was overjoyed at her radiance and impressed by her courage to come forward.

Without saying anything to the false bride, the king ordered a great feast. The prince sat in the middle and the princess sat on one side, while the false bride sat on the other. So radiant was the princess that the waiting maid did not recognize her. After they had their fill, the king said he would tell them a tale. So he began, and he told everything the princess had told him as though it were a story he had once heard. At the end, he asked the false bride what should be done with one who would behave thus. The false bride replied, "That girl deserves to have her head chopped off and nailed to the dark gates of the city!"

"Thou art she!" exclaimed the old king, "and thou hast judged thyself! So shall it be done to thee!" So away went the false bride at the order of the king.

The prince then married the true princess, and at the wedding the good fairy came and restored Falada to life. From then on, they reigned over the kingdom in peace and happiness all their lives.

ACCEPTANCE IN MAGIC

The power to accept, the widdershins power of the west, is your starting point as you journey inward toward your spiritual center. Neopagan magical systems infuse every aspect of life with symbolic value and in this case, the west symbolizes endings. After all, the sun goes down in the west; daily the symbolic connection between the west and endings is played in the heavens.

One day ends so that another can begin. So to pagans, endings are really doorways or transition points to something new. If you apply this symbol to your magic, to your change in consciousness, the west represents the transitional stage that occurs within you when you shift from a focus on the outer world to the inner world through meditation. Meditation is like alchemy in that it transforms the deosil power to dare into the widdershins power to accept.

The power to dare indicates courage. It signifies the ability to magically go beyond limitations and boundaries. But in order to do this, it is useful to know of what the boundaries consist. How high are the mountains you climb? How swift is the wind that blows on your back? What exactly are your parameters?

The power to accept is the power to get grounded or anchored in the moment—in temporal and spatial reality—to get a clear understanding of your personal limitations as well as your advantages. When you accept, you clearly and uncompromisingly assess your life in the moment. When you acquire this power, you root your spiritual growth on firm ground. It allows you to get real and view the here and now as it is—not as you want it to be, nor as others describe it.

The power to accept also delineates your personal boundaries, which are the limits that define who you are. Once you clearly understand these boundaries, you open yourself to see the magical pathways across them. In other words, you can create a new set of boundaries.

If you need 400 dollars each month to cover your expenses and you only earn 100, then accepting the reality of your financial situation can guide you toward the actions necessary to cover the rest of your expenses. Obviously, 100 is not 400, and to live without acceptance of that reality can keep you in straitened circumstances. When you don't evoke the power to accept, you deny the specifics of your environment, of your needs, goals, and aspirations—all of which guide magic. What good is it to cast a spell without knowing the spell's purpose? The spell's purpose—its focus—represents this idea of boundaries.

Magic without acceptance, without parameters, is as pointless as a beginning a journey without knowing either where you are right now or where you are going. In the Western tradition, magical journeys start where you are now and end in a place you had planned to go.

Acceptance begins by honestly assessing yourself and your life right now. In other words, consider what it is that can be measured, seen, heard, tasted, smelled, or felt; know what it is that you are feeling emotionally; be aware of your thought processes, and you are on your way to attaining the first of the four dark moon powers.

Getting a handle on time and place is a good way to help you evoke the magical powers of acceptance.

Application of "The Goose Girl"

The tale of the Goose Girl starkly illustrates the process that begins when anyone chooses to ignore or reject reality—and consequently chooses not to move into action. The Goose Girl, once a lovely little princess who held tremendous promise, gradually lost her dignity, her horse, her clothes, and finally her own identity.

Your identity is not solely who you *were*, nor is it who you *will be*; it is who you *are* now. Without accepting this moment in time, you can become like the Goose Girl and lose your immediate sense of identity. Furthermore, in the tale, the impudent waiting maid threatened to kill the princess should she ever take action or speak out against her. For us, the present moment can feel threatening, and just like the waiting maid, it may paralyze us with fear. When you do not accept what is happening in the moment you lose power because you cannot act effectively.

The tale does not leave you with the negative message; it goes on to show what happens when you claim the power to accept. At that moment your life is infused with power; it becomes balanced and transformed. The power behind acceptance is its ability to cue you into the actions that need to be taken in the moment.

In that final crucial moment of the story, when the Goose Girl takes action and tells the king of her plight, the story tells us that she was transformed; she was so radiant "that she was beyond recognition." Acknowledgement of the situation empowered the Goose Girl to act, and so transformed her present condition. Acceptance transforms you as well, for when you live your life in the current moment, you move from a consciousness of passivity to that of activity. You then act out of your power.

The Sage speaks:

Know now this mystery: timing is all in the ways of magic. My teachers pointed out the significance of the ebbs and flows of energy that occurred with time's passage. Magic moves with nothing more than the moon, the stars, the sun, the tides, the earth. But the mystery is that timing exists within you as well.

You have a season within. Some folk are in their summer while others are in winter, just as surely as some folk experience joy while others are in their despair. But know this well: there is no season or time more important than that which is now. You are only given the present to do with as you will. The present is your point of power.

TIME

Joseph Campbell points out that "time is but a reference"[1] that refers to an experience of our consciousness. It is a symbol that describes what is going on in the here and now in our bodies, minds, or spirits. Pagans use the seasons to symbolize what is going on at any of their three levels of existence. In other words, each of us is experiencing a "season" that is a metaphor for experiences, feelings, thoughts, and emotions.

For instance, if I am in a time of my life that calls for deep reflection, I might say that my mind is in a *fall* period. Or if I am interested in beginning an exercise program, I might say that my body is in a *spring* time, a time for physical renewal.

Knowing your season in body, mind, or spirit helps ground you into present time and into your power of acceptance. The exercises to come will help you discover your season and your power.

Time Exercise

Make a list of actions, thoughts, and feelings that you associate with the keywords listed below. Write down the words that come into your mind without editing them. Do this exercise as quickly as possible and allow yourself to be spontaneous. It is not important to fill in all of the blanks.

Keyword: *Winter*

Winter *actions*: What kind of body movements suggest "winter?" (E.g.: slow, sharp, quick, etc.)

1. stiff
2. lethargic
3. plodding
4. encumbered
5. heavy
6.
7.
8.
9.
10.
11.
12.
13.
14.
15.

Winter *thoughts*: What are the thoughts that go through your mind at winter time?

1. inside
2. withdrawn
3. quiet
4. depressive
5. stagnant
6. burdened
7. weighted
8. taxes
9. stale
10.
11.
12.
13.
14.
15.

Winter *feelings*: What are the emotions you associate with winter?

1. depressive
2. mourning
3. death
4. burdened
5. cold
6. cozy
7. hibernating
8. squrrel energy
9.
10.
11.
12.
13.
14.
15.

Keyword: *Spring*

Spring *actions*: What kind of body movements suggest "spring?"
(E.g.: lyrical, smooth, etc.)

1. light
2. energetic
3. renewed
4. reenergized
5. alive
6.
7.
8.
9.
10.
11.
12.
13.
14.
15.

Spring *thoughts*: What are the thoughts that go through your mind at spring time?

1. outside
2. preparation
3. ending of mourning
4. reaching outward
5.
6.
7.
8.
9.
10.
11.
12.
13.
14.
15.

Spring *feelings*: What are the emotions you associate with spring?

1. uplifted
2. hopeful
3. optimistic
4. refreshed
5. ending hibernation
6. warmth
7. excitement
8.
9.
10.
11.
12.
13.
14.
15.

Keyword: *Summer*

Summer *actions*: What kind of body movements suggest "summer?"
(E.g.: quick, lively, etc.)

1. consistent
2. active
3. busy
4.
5.
6.
7.
8.
9.
10.
11.
12.
13.
14.
15.

Summer *thoughts*: What are the thoughts that go through your mind at summer time?

1. responsibilities
2. too many options
3. overly bright
4. always on
5.
6.
7.
8.
9.
10.
11.
12.
13.
14.
15.

Summer *feelings*: What are the emotions you associate with summer?

1. inhaling   6.   11.
2. options   7.   12.
3. relaxing   8.   13.
4.   9.   14.
5.   10.   15.

Keyword: *Fall*

Fall *actions*: What kind of body movements suggest "fall?" (E.g.: stillness, unfolding, etc.)

1. chop wood   6. preparations   11.
2. rake leaves   7.   12.
3. crisp air   8.   13.
4. definition of   9.   14.
5. self & cold air   10.   15.

Fall *thoughts*: What are the thoughts that go through your mind at fall time?

1. scholastic   6.   11.
2. intellect   7.   12.
3. holiday prep.   8.   13.
4.   9.   14.
5.   10.   15.

Fall *feelings*: What are the emotions you associate with fall?

1. grieving winters   6.   11.
2. advance   7.   12.
3. closure   8.   13.
4. goodbye   9.   14.
5.   10.   15.

Now, take a look at each of the categories and decide which season best symbolizes your personal "time" at this moment in body, mind, and spirit. For the body or physical realm, begin with the "actions" lists. For the mind level, read the "thoughts" lists. For your season of spirit, look over the feelings lists.[2]

Which one of the three lists (actions, thoughts, feelings) did you have the most difficulty completing? Whichever it was accents the level of being with which you are least connected. You need to concentrate on evoking the power to accept at this level.

Which one of the three lists was easiest to complete? Whichever it was highlights the level of being with which you are most connected.

The Sage speaks:

Wishing for snow while living in a desert is a fool's game. Know where you are, and that will tell you what you can and cannot do in the present time. If you are in the east, expect a sunrise—if in the west, a sunset. When you are in water, you must be wet. These are all laws of place.

PLACE

Place is important in gaining the power to accept because, just like time, place can be a symbol for what goes on within any of your three levels of being. This means you can infuse your place—right where you are now—with magical meaning that will in turn teach you something about yourself. For instance, if I am living in a place (an apartment, house, condo, etc.) that I characterize as "happy and stimulating," it is a reflection of my own consciousness. I have absorbed the details of my place through my physical senses, and then interpreted them, allowing my unconscious to make associations. The associations it has made correlate with the terms "happy and stimulating." The result is that my consciousness will be moved in the direction of happiness and stimulation as long as I am in that place, or until I change my mind about the character of my place.

Characterizing the immediate place was a common practice among various ancient tribal cultures. An example of this practice occurred among the Icelandic people. They had a custom called "land naming" or "land taking" through which they would recognize in the local landscape images from their mythology. Any new or unfamiliar land would quickly became theirs when they infused it with their sacred imagery.[3] For people of contemporary Western cultures, this practice needs some adaptation.

The difference in this practice for Westerners comes from the fact that our culture does not have a coherent mythology that binds our sacred vision into a spiritual collective like ancient tribal peoples. We are taught to honor our autonomy in all ways. We are encouraged to explore our personal pantheon, personal vision, and personal myth that can guide us on our journey toward power. What guides the practice of land naming is our personal vision or mythologization. It is not the symbols of our collective culture that aid in our transformation, but the symbols that spring from our personal unconscious, our personal lives and experiences.

For your magical purposes, the practice of land naming is called "place naming." Through it you will not claim the landscape as much as the landscape or place will claim you. In essence, it will become a metaphor that describes where you are in body, mind, or spirit.

Place Naming Exercise

The power to accept begins with self-acceptance, and this exercise opens the doorway for that to begin.

As you did in the time exercise, begin by answering each question quickly to avoid editing from your critical faculties. Be spontaneous and creative with your answers—spontaneity is the life blood of magic.

1. Name the place where you spend the majority of your time (home, office, outdoors, etc.).

2. Name the place where you spend the second most amount of time.

3. Use descriptive words and brief phrases to characterize each place (light, bright, happy, dirty, dingy, etc.).

   Place #1 adjectives:
   peaceful, organized, orderly, serene

Place #2 adjectives:

busy, peaceful, meditative, reflectful, heaven

4. The adjectives you chose to describe these places are words that represent aspects of yourself. In light of the descriptions you've come up with, think of how they reflect your being on one or more levels.

Note: *In this part of the exercise you can slow down. It is important to make conscious connections between the words and your levels of being.*

Physical level (e.g., "These places make me feel physically drained" or "They stimulate me and get me going," etc.):

Mental level (e.g., "These places make me feel confused," or "These places help keep my thoughts in order," etc.):

Emotional/Spiritual level (e.g., "It makes me feel happy," or "These places make me feel afraid," etc.):

Listed below are some of the traditional Wiccan associations with time and place. Read the following listings and try to associate these times and places with your three levels of being.

Time: *Spring and Dawn*   **Place:** *East*
Keyword: *Initiation*

When you are symbolically in a time of spring/dawn or in the east in our lives, you are experiencing renewal. Ideas, thoughts and communications are just beginning to bud. Spring is a time for hope, for looking forward and making plans. Are you starting something new? Are you having new thoughts? Are you honing your communication skills? Then you are in the spring, dawn, or east.

Time: *Summer and Midday*   **Place:** *South*
Keyword: *Action*

When you are symbolically in a time of summer/midday or in the
south in your life, you are experiencing fruition. Fruition means that
whatever you've planted is coming to full blossom, beneficially or
otherwise. Plans made in the spring/dawn/east stage are carried out
at this time. Summer brings into action the promises of spring.
Whatever was hoped for, planned for, and dreamed of comes to pass
in the summer's time. Are you in a time of fulfillment? Are you
beginning to take action? Are you experiencing tremendous energy?
Then you are in your summer, midday, or south.

Time: *Fall and Dusk*   **Place:** *West*
Keyword: *Reaping*

When you are symbolically in a time of fall/dusk or in the west in
your life, you are experiencing a time of harvest. It is a time and a
place of collecting the fruits of one's plans of spring and actions of
summer. The west is a place of endings and of deep emotions. Are
you reaping the rewards for your plans and actions? Are you becoming introspective or emotional? Are things coming to an end? Then
you are in your fall, dusk, or west.

Time: *Winter and Midnight*   **Place:** *North*
Keyword: *Silence and mystery*

Winter, midnight, and the north bring about inertia, stillness, and
silence. All things proceed from the stillness of the void and to that all
things return. "Like a drop of water, flowing to the ocean," is how one
pagan chant states this principle.[4] Winter is also the time of dearth,
lack, and repose. Are you experiencing stillness? Is there a hint of
mystery in your life? Are you taking time out to recuperate and rest?
Then you are in your winter, midnight, or north.

The Chalice Rite

The chalice is the magical tool of the west in traditional Wicca. For this exercise, find a chalice or special cup that you would like to use only for magical or sacred workings. Fill the cup with water and take it to a quiet place that faces the west. While sitting, focus your attention on the cup. Take note of how the cup forms the limits or boundaries of the water. The cup shapes the water and gives it form. Imagine what the cup is in your life. In other words, what are your limits and what are your assets? After a few moments of pondering this, hold the cup up high toward the west and say: *I welcome thee, powers of the widdershins west. I embrace the power to accept!*

Meditation: Gaining the Power To Accept

Close your eyes and take several deep slow breaths. Be present with each inhale and each exhale. Do you inhale fast or slow, hard or soft? Do you exhale fast or slow, hard or soft? Pay attention to each breath as you continue to deeply breathe.

Allow a blue mist to swirl around your body, starting at your feet and surrounding you completely to the top of your head. This mist will begin to lift you and take you to a sacred place and a sacred time.

[**Partner: pause for a moment.**]

Invite the mist to set you down now, for you have arrived at a sacred grove of oak trees. The trees stand in a ring, and the center is covered with long grass. The time is dusk; the sun has already set, but there is sufficient light to see well. The sky is purple, dotted with a few visible sparkling stars. The moon is on the eastern horizon.

In the center of the oak-tree grove is a large, egg-shaped mirror. From the trees in the west, your wisdom self, the inner crone or sage, enters the ring of trees. This guide takes you by the hand to the cosmic mirror. As you stand before it, the surface of the mirror swirls and clouds, but then an image emerges and the truth of who you are and what you are right now in time and place is revealed. What do you see? Next, a single word will emerge that describes what and who you are. What is that word?

When you have seen this, the vision clears from the mirror and the surface clouds over once again. Your spirit guide leaves you now by the west once again. The blue mist swirls around you, lifts you up and takes you back to your body. When you are fully back inside your body, take a moment to contemplate this experience.

Notes

1. In this quote, Joseph Campbell is expanding on the line from Johann Wolfgang von Goethe's *Faust*, "Alles Vergangliche ist nur ein Gleichnis" (Everything transitory is but a reference). See, e.g., Joseph Campbell, *The Inner Reaches of Outer Space*, New York: Harper & Row, 1986, p. 115.

2. The choice to connect feelings with emotions was conscious on my part. Thoughts are manifestations of the mind. Actions are manifestations of the body, and both of these levels can be intentionally controlled. We have access to them in such a way that we can manipulate them directly. Feelings are properly spiritual because they are a quality, a product that emerges from experiences of the mind and the body. They are the invisible undercurrent that drives us. That is not to say that emotions are what make up spirit. This was a purely symbolic correlation.

3. Joseph Campbell (Betty Sue Flowers, ed.), *The Power of Myth*, New York: Doubleday, 1988, p. 94.

4. This comes from the chant "We All Come from the Goddess," based on a chant by Richard Quinn and also attributed to Z. Budapest. See, e.g., Barbara Ardinger, *A Woman's Book of Rituals and Celebrations*, San Rafael: New World Library, 1992, p. 41.

Chapter 7

The Power to Surrender

The Sage speaks:

A flower can only grow as fast as it is capable of growing. There is no sense in hurrying the flower. This may be obvious to you, yet at times I see you trying to convince the flowers otherwise! Surrender to the flower's process so that a bloom may finally come to pass, my child. It is this same rule that governs life, love, and magic. In magic, however, you are the one who decides what seeds to plant and where they will be planted. The rest is in the hands of the Mighty Ones.

As you continue on the journey through the widdershins spiral, your next stop is in the south. Traditional Neopagan magical systems associate the south with the element of fire, which holds *the power to will*. The ability to manifest desires through directing psychic energy is the power to will. In widdershins work, the power of willing transforms into the power to surrender, which shifts your magical focus from fire itself to that which fuels the fire—from energy itself to the source of energy.

When something burns, it surrenders to fire. Every fire burns because it is fueled from some source. Similarly, every physical form that contains life is fueled by spirit. This sounds very basic, but it is important to keep in mind because it translates into magical work. In order for magic to be alive, it too must be infused with spirit. Surrendering or linking to the realm of spirit is the power that underlies willing.

In practical terms, through surrendering you tap the source of energy behind the power to will and learn to release it. The dark moon power of surrendering is all about release. Initially, this power allows you to release and relax physically and mentally, so that you can access the source power of spirit. This then allows an unimpeded flow of psychic energy.

Once you have physically, mentally, and spiritually surrendered and power begins to flow, you can tap back into the deosil power of fire (to will) in order to mystically and physically direct the flow of spiritual energy. Directing spiritual energy sounds mysterious or even difficult to do, but it can be as simple as performing a physical action. Physical action is spirit energy in motion. Physical action helps move spiritual energy into manifestation. There is no sense in praying that your car will start up when it is out of gas. In that moment, action is needed—fill up the tank! Spiral within to tap the source of power, then spiral back out into action—that is the key to powerful magic. It is a balancing act.

Magical work requires flexibility of consciousness on the part of the Witch or shaman because spiritual energy moves fluidly. If you become rigid by anchoring your consciousness to either pole of willing or surrendering, it is difficult to generate magical power. It is impossible to sustain a flow of energy through willing if the psychic channels are not opened through surrendering. If you stay at the pole of willing, you can begin to drain your personal psychic faculties because you have not accessed spirit, which is the source of all power.

Likewise, too much surrendering opens the way to apathy. You can open yourself to gross intemperance and debauchery if you release yourself beyond the limits of self-control. Spiraling within opens the pathway for spiritual energy to emerge; spiraling back out opens the pathway for action. This double spiral of power helps to keep you flexible between the two poles. Surrendering is not only a magical, spiritual method, it is also a way of being in the world. It is a psychological position of seeing the processes of nature as complete—as needing no help to further it along. Mainstream westerners find this a difficult power to assume because their spiritual systems support the notion that the world and humanity are fallen, corrupt, or sinful. When the world is viewed as a mistake, it cannot be valued beyond its potential to be exploited. This is the mindset of control. It elicits *power over* the world, which is the usual way western culture teaches us to access power. "Power over" is a patriarchal construct, and it needs hierarchy—a pecking order—to keep it alive. It is dominance over nature and over others.[1]

If you surrender to the world and to nature, you open your consciousness to the realization that humans are, as Native American Chief Seattle once described, "strands in the web of life" and not the entire web. Whatever it is we do to this web, we do to ourselves. Through this perspective, you evoke the power and strength that comes from interdependence. A new power paradigm emerges, called *power with*, when you surrender to interdependence. This power does not rely on hierarchy for efficacy. "Power with" turns hierarchy on its side, so that empowerment is evenly distributed; each of us and every creation has something valuable to offer in our existence and therefore holds a certain amount of the power of the whole.[2]

For example, there is power in a support network of friends because of the collaboration of skills and resources that go beyond the capabilities of an individual. An individual will is necessary at times, but so is a collective one. The power to surrender is a power that helps ground you in a perspective of mutual cooperation, which is well beyond the bounds of the individual authoritarianism that patriarchy supports.[3]

Again, there is danger in clinging solely to this psychological perspective. There are times when individual action is necessary. For example, in the cases of self-protection, improvement, and realization, or to fulfill a personal desire, you must mobilize your individual will and move into action. As with the powers of the west (to accept and to dare), the Witch learns to balance the south's powers of willing and surrendering.

Quarrelsome Demyan

Once there was a man named Demyan who loved to pick fights. Everyone in the village knew of this characteristic, so they tried their best to avoid the man.

The villagers did such a good job keeping Demyan at bay that he became frustrated because he could no longer pick fights openly. So he began to resort to trickery. One day he invited another villager into his house. Once the villager was inside, Demyan told his wife to set the table, and he asked his guest to sit down for supper. The guest politely said to Demyan, "You shouldn't have gone to so much trouble."

With that Demyan slapped the man in the face and said, "Always obey the master when you're in his house!" The guest, falling for the trick, sat down, and when the host offered him food, he ate.

Soon into the meal Demyan began to cut countless slices of bread. The guest asked, "Why do you cut so much bread, Demyan?"

Demyan gave the guest another slap, saying, "It is impolite to give advice to the host! Obey the master when you're in his house." The guest became distraught. When Demyan offered him some bread, the guest refused to eat, thus disobeying Demyan, who kept beating him, saying, "In someone else's house, obey the master!" The guest fled from Demyan's house beaten and upset.

Soon after that, a shabbily dressed man rode up to the house on an old horse. Without being invited, he entered Demyan's front gate and rode into the yard. Demyan thought to himself, "Aha! Another guest to thrash!" "Welcome, stranger," said Demyan.

"Thank you, Demyan," said the stranger, "but please forgive me for having come without first asking permission."

"Never mind that, come in, you are welcome here!"

The stranger entered Demyan's house and was entreated to sit down at the table. Soon, Demyan commanded his wife to serve the dishes of food and to bring the bread. The fellow ate and ate without contradicting his host. No matter how much Demyan tried to provoke his guest, he could not find a pretext for striking him.

Finally, frustrated beyond words, Demyan decided to resort to trickier tricks. He brought out his very best clothes and told the stranger, "Take off what you are wearing and put this on." Demyan, expecting the stranger to refuse out of politeness, was shocked when the fellow did not refuse. The stranger put on the clothes that his host gave him. Demyan began to offer the stranger this and that around the house, but still the man would not quarrel.

Demyan brought out his best horse, saddled it with his best silver gear, put the gold bridle on the horse, and said to his guest, "Take my horse. Yours is poor looking and ungroomed." Demyan expected the man would surely refuse, but the fellow mounted the horse. Frustrated beyond his limits, Demyan finally told the guest to ride forth. The fellow urged the horse on, rode out of the yard, and disappeared down the road. Demyan followed the man with his eyes, clapped his hands, and said, "Well, at last I've found my equal! Not he, but I was fooled. I wanted to thrash him, but instead I lost my horse!"[4]

Application of "Quarrelsome Demyan"

The two dinner guests in the fairy tale of Quarrelsome Demyan illustrate well the polar spiraling paths through the power of fire. Demyan represents what cannot (and should not) be controlled—namely, nature.[5] The first guest to Demyan's house symbolizes the impotence of willing against the tide of nature. We cannot prevent the sun from rising or setting, nor the moon from waxing or waning.

Yet in that tale, the visitor tries over and over to master, control, and will the situation. The result is a beating. Every time he exerts his will against the tide of Demyan, he is struck. This is the predicament our world faces today. In effect, nature is rebelling right now due to human attempts to control it. Ozone depletion, hunger, and disease are some of the ways nature has slapped back at human control.

The first guest would have claimed much more control over the situation had he surrendered or harmonized with Demyan. He needed to cooperate with the prevailing energies. The second visitor of the tale utilizes the power of surrendering to his advantage. Because he opened to that prevailing tide and surrendered to it, Demyan's second visitor was ultimately able to gain a form of power. He claimed a new horse and new clothes, which symbolizes the idea that we too can gain power through harmonizing with nature's tides.

The Sage Speaks:

When fire is set ablaze across a wide, grassy field, it cannot be contained. No, the entire field, every blade of grass, offers itself to the life-changing influences of the fire. After it is touched by the flame, that grass becomes something else over time, something that is needed by the field at that moment. Like the grass, surrender yourself to the processes of fire and embrace your perfect place in the universe.

Each of the following exercises will aid you in surrendering on each of the three levels of being. Try them in a series and then monitor your results. Through these exercises, you should experience a feeling of clarity and harmoniousness.

SURRENDERING THE BODY

Find a drumming audiotape or have a magical partner play live drums for this exercise. Some excellent drum tapes to use are recorded by Gabrielle Roth and Jim McGrath.[6] You can find these artists' works in any well-stocked music store.

Practice this exercise on the last night of the dark moon, which symbolizes the moon's "surrender" of light. Just as the moon has, in essence, surrendered its body, so will you. For this work, you need a work space that is relatively open, so that you don't bump into things as you engage in physical surrendering.

To begin, find a drum rhythm that encourages movement. Select one that has a consistent beat. Then stand (or sit) in the center of your work space. Ground yourself in time and place and then focus on feeling the weight of your body. Become conscious of the pull of gravity.

As you do this, listen to the drumming. Allow the pulsating rhythm to sweep over your body, and allow it to begin moving your toes. Stay with that movement for a moment. What surprises do your toes reveal as they move? Next, add in your feet. How do your feet respond to the rhythm? How do the toes and feet move together?

Slowly, add in each part of your body to this dance of release—your knees, upper thigh, hips, stomach, chest, shoulders, arms, elbows, fingers, neck, and finally, add in your head. Be sure to spend a moment or two with each body part as you add it into the dance. The final, complete movement should be spontaneous and wild; the experience should be ecstatic and transformative.

I have done this exercise with many different people and occasionally there are those who balk because they feel shame over their bodies, or they have fears about moving or dancing in front of other people. Yet, amazingly, once they complete the exercise, they feel exhilarated and liberated. The moment of transformation comes when they move beyond their doubts and fears.

Many of them ask me why they had been afraid for so long to let go. I tell them that it is because they had learned to identify only with the parts of themselves that were culturally accepted. These were the parts that only dwelt in the light—the parts that said, "You can only move your body like everyone else, otherwise you should be ashamed of yourself." Through the exercise of body surrendering, the dark moon or unknown parts were what emerged.

When you fear the dark, fear of letting go is a certainty.

Consciousness Surrender

Experiencing surrender at the level of the mind is what I call wondering. This is the widdershins power of the east, which you will explore more fully in the next chapter. However, this exercise gives you a taste—a small preview—of this power.

This exercise is good to do any time you experience lack of clarity in your thought processes. Begin by finding a comfortable body position, either sitting or standing. Close your eyes and take several deep, slow breaths while imagining that your muscles all melt like butter; they become soft and pliable.

Travel into your head and imagine how all of your thoughts look. Give them all sizes, colors, and shapes—just make it all up! Then, imagine that you are able to open wide a doorway in the front of your head. You can see that on the other side of this doorway it is clear and sunny. Now imagine that all of the different sizes, shapes, and colors jump out of the doorway. Allow this to continue until nothing is left.

Then imagine that a gentle breeze picks up and blows through you. When you are ready, open your eyes.

Spirit Energy Release

Now that you have successfully surrendered in body and mind, you are ready to tap into the dimension of spirit and release its energies.

Begin by finding a comfortable position, either sitting or standing. Again take several slow, deep breaths. Breath is important in generating spiritual energy,[7] so make sure your breathing is slow, deep, and controlled throughout the exercise.

As you breathe, imagine that flames encircle you. They are a few feet away at first, but you feel their heat. The flames start to move in now. They continue their approach until they are literally at your feet. The flames do not hurt; they simply impart a warm, tingling sensation. Take a deep breath and allow yourself to feel the tingling and warmth.

Suddenly, the flames climb your legs, and you feel the tingling sensation directly on your body. Surrender to this. Allow these flames to climb up and cover your stomach, then your chest, arms, neck, and head. Surrender to the power of fire. Let it transform you. Look through your spirit eyes and see the world through the center of the flames. Meld with the flames. Become the flames. Allow them to burn away your physical being to reveal that part of you which is immortal. Continue to breathe deeply.

At this point, begin to breathe in the power of the fire. With each in-drawn breath, fill up your body with this energy. Imagine that you are hollow inside and that an orange-red light fills up the space with each inward breath. As you do this, notice that the flames outside your body die down. They are being absorbed into your spirit. Continue to draw in the power of the fire as you feel your legs fill with its warmth and tingling light. Then your hips and stomach swell with power. Soon your chest and arms expand with fire power. Finally, your neck and your head fill up with the energy of fire.

When you are ready, open your eyes. Move into action and direct the psychic energy toward some goal. Be sure to ground and center yourself after this exercise.

The Athame Ritual

This exercise makes use of the athame (pronounced: ah-tha'-may), one of the Witch's most powerful personal tools. Traditional Wiccan lore says that the athame is a black-handled, double-edged knife. The athame directs the will of the magical practitioner.

In this exercise, the athame symbolically connects your personal will to the rest of nature.

Items Needed:

- An athame or some other sharp blade.
- A red taper candle (in a holder).

On the first night of the waning moon, use your athame to make fourteen evenly spaced notches along the length of the red taper candle. Then light the taper and watch the flame consume the wax and wick. As you watch, realize that the candle surrenders to the flame. It does not resist. It surrenders its present form and transforms itself into light, heat, and warmth. The candle's potential becomes actualized as it surrenders. Once the candle burns the wax down to the first notch, extinguish the flame with the blade of the athame. You can do this by patting the flame down.

Continue this meditation each night for the remaining thirteen nights of the waning moon.

On the last night, after you have lit the remaining candle and have watched it burn down, take your athame and go outdoors.

Face the south and hold the blade up to the black, moonless sky. Then with both of your hands, plunge the blade into the earth and say: *I welcome thee powers of the widdershins south. I embrace the power to surrender!*

Meditation:

Gaining the Power to Surrender

Close your eyes and take several deep, slow breaths. With each breath, allow your body to become still. With each breath, quiet your mind. With each breath, imagine that you move closer to the center of your being. Mentally travel through your body, from your toes to your head, and relax each part as you go along.

When you have finished, imagine that a blue mist begins to swirl around your feet. It moves upward and covers you completely. The mist is warm and comforting. Soon, it begins to lift you up and take you on a journey to a place of learning.

[**Partner: pause for a moment.**]

The mist sets you down now, and it dissipates. As it does, it reveals a new scene. You find yourself in front of a large oak tree in the middle of a warm, sunny field. Take note of its immense size. Walk close to it. Touch it. As you do, notice that your hand slips easily into the tree, as though it was an illusion. Let your arm go inside, then allow the rest of your body to follow, until you are completely inside the oak tree.

Suddenly, a transformation takes place. Your arms become branches and leaves, your feet become roots—you become the oak tree. Imagine how it feels to have branches and leaves. Feel your root system in the earth below you. Imagine how you take in nutrients from the soil and clear, still water from underground springs.

Now, feel the warmth of the sun on your leaves. A wind picks up now and sways your branches. Feel the rush of the breeze as it moves your body.

Time begins to speed up now; the sun moves fast through the sky, and soon it is dark outside. Look up and feel the cool light of the waning moon and stars on your leaves, branches, and trunk.

Just as suddenly as before, another transformation takes place, and you find yourself back outside of the tree. Look at it again and know that its life is not independent. Its life falls into a vast web of interdependency that reaches into the deepest parts of the universe. See now how the web sustains your life.

[Partner: pause for a moment.]

The blue mist swirls at your feet, climbs, and covers you again. It lifts you and brings you back to the place where you began the journey. It takes you back to your physical body. When you are fully back, open your eyes. Take a moment to assimilate the experience.

Notes

1. Starhawk, *Truth or Dare*, San Francisco: Harper and Row, 1987, p. 9.

2. For a full explanation of this, see, e.g., His Holiness the Dali Lama, *A Policy of Kindness: An Anthology of Writings by and about the Dali Lama*, New York: Snow Lion, 1990.

3. Starhawk illustrates these types of power as they relate to group dynamics. However, they are applicable to the flows and directions of spiritual power. See, e.g., Starhawk, *Truth or Dare*, San Francisco: Harper and Row, 1987, pp. 8–10.

4. Based on translation of "Quarrelsome Demyan" by Norbert Guterman in Aleksandr Afanasev, *Russian Fairy Tales*, New York: Pantheon Books, 1945, pp. 163–164.

5. Many of the Russian fairy tales I encountered had a focus on combat. Although their characters many times represent spiritual principles, oddly, they are armed and ready for battle.

6. Some titles of drumming tapes by Gabrielle Roth that I recommend for this work are *Totem, Bones,* and *Luna.* The titles that I like for Jim McGrath are *Drum Spirit* and *Percussive Environments.*

7. Actually the origin of the word spirit is the Latin *spiritus,* which literally means, "breathing," "breath," or "the breath of life." See, e.g., D.P. Simpson, *Cassell's Latin and English Dictionary,* New York: MacMillan Publishing, 1987.

Chapter 8

The Power to Wonder

The Sage speaks:

Fear not to become a fool, for fools dare to go beyond what is known. All of what you know today becomes meaningless in the face of tomorrow. Remember that it was once common knowledge that the sun, the planets, and all of the universe made passage around the earth! Fools dared to move beyond that knowledge. It is your task as well, to move beyond the realm of what is known into what will be known. Step off the precipice, my sweet fool, and tumble into uncharted territory, for the power to wonder lies in waiting there.

Beginning to Wonder

"I wonder." I seem to be caught often with that saying on my lips. My wondering doesn't come from my having little knowledge, but instead from my learning the value of releasing the knowledge I've invested in over the years. This may sound quite paradoxical or even foolish, and in fact it is.

Those who possess the power to wonder align with the energy of the fool. True fools are not necessarily people with little intelligence, nor are they irresponsible, flighty, or dumb. They are wise enough to know that in order to conceptualize creatively, they must let go of what is already known. When they do so, they may bring back a new idea, a healing elixir, or a renewed teaching, but we can be assured that its origin is always in the unknown. That's where fools dare to go.

Someone who wonders has the ability to experience life through a consciousness that holds a certain suppleness. This fool's consciousness is able to get beyond the threshold guardians who halt all others with the words, "It can't be done." But fools know that it can be done, given enough time and enough space to wonder.

Those who cannot accept change or diversity are those who fear wonderers. A certain amount of diversity is actually needed in order for organic life to flourish. Anything that stands motionless, frozen in time and space, becomes devoid of the life flow, the mana or chi that pervades all matter. When you wonder, you open to your highest creativity; you open to your deepest self-expression. This is the next phase in the process of moving into your inward life, of spiraling widdershins.

You began in the west with grounding and centering your consciousness in the here and now, then in the south you learned to relax and allow the process of the universe to take over in body and mind. Now you will open to the spontaneity of your consciousness.

The following puzzle illustrates the idea of flexibility of consciousness, wondering, and moving beyond the limits:

Instructions: Connect all nine diamonds using only four straight connecting lines. Do not lift your pen from the page as you draw the four lines.

The key to solving this puzzle lies in your willingness to challenge assumptions.

An example of widespread assumptive thinking is in the form of what I call the "cultural map." This map is a set of unspoken rules that govern our social behavior and keep us in line. For instance, you may know that you are going against the cultural map by staring at a stranger, or by talking about sexual behavior in public. Others around us help to keep us in conformity with the map as well. The map is all around us at all times. The insidious power of social inculcation is that it often operates below the level of awareness; many times it is difficult to detect, let alone escape completely. Placing yourself into the mindset of wondering helps you to break from influences that operate below your levels of awareness.

The puzzle, then, is not one of logic so much as it is of letting go of the known and venturing into the unknown. To solve the puzzle you must venture outside the boundaries of the square of diamonds:

In Wicca, the deosil eastern direction symbolizes the power to know. The east aligns with the element air in this system, and air symbolizes thought, communication, ideas, and knowledge. Air symbolizes these categories because of their intangible qualities. You cannot see the air, yet it exists; you cannot see thoughts, yet you know they exist. Knowledge, then, is the primary power evoked in the deosil spiral. However, there are times when the strictures of knowledge cannot meet your needs. At those moments it is time to spiral into the dark, into your widdershins power of the east.

The dark is what is unknown or not yet revealed. What we do not know we begin to wonder about. Wondering can lead to knowing, but wondering is itself a magical power. Remember that power comes from the life force (to Pagans, it is the Goddess and the God), and the life force is movement. Another way of saying this is: movement is life. Wondering is the movement of the mind, and it is the true power underlying our ability to know. When you spiral inward and adopt the power of wondering, you begin to claim a liberating consciousness. In essence, you become liberated from the limits of knowledge through this third of the dark moon powers.

In magical systems, it is not wise to be too sure about what it is you seem to know. Knowledge spins around quickly, only to become obsolete. What was knowledge yesterday is seen as quaint naivete today. Knowledge is a temporal manifestation; it is based on the consensus of a society, directed by social interests and concerns. In other words, we have all agreed, generation after generation, that a certain body of knowledge is valuable and worth obtaining.

However, this kind of knowledge can decay quickly. For instance, our history shifts daily under our feet. The once supposedly solid ground of history is today beginning to resemble quicksand, for an entire generation of new historians, microhistorians, and deconstructionists, look at events gone by from entirely new, revisionist perspectives.

Traditionally history is told from the perspective of the winners. However, these new historians create an infinite number of possible histories by taking the perspective of the underdogs, or outsiders, thus connecting events into new strings of meaning. These historians are true fools; they have dared to go beyond the bounds of what was once called fact and brought forth the awaiting potential.

The power to wonder places your consciousness at the center point of pure potential. The ground is shifty in such a position, but an entire spectrum of possibilities is open to the wonderer. Imagination is the key to wondering. Imagination is the key to magic. Use of the imagination is a job requirement for Witches and shamans. The imagination helps us to move with the flow of nature, with our instincts and intuition.

The unconscious is the realm of instinct, and when you allow instinct to take over, you are driven by forces beyond your immediate comprehension. Your consciousness becomes freed up, and new possibilities and directions are open to you when you wonder.

Balance is the key to magical practices, so keep in mind that in the east, too much wondering can lead to a kind of self-delusion. To regain your bearings, remember that on the compass wheel, the balance point of the east is the west, which holds the power to accept. If you find yourself becoming consistently ungrounded and wondering too far beyond practicality, go back to Chapter 6 and practice the grounding exercises.

The Boy Who Did Not Know How to Shudder

Long before there was any time, there lived a father and his son. The father so loved his child that over the years, he kept careful watch, never letting any harm come to him, nor allowing anyone to say a word in anger. The lad grew into a handsome youth, but one who was not learned in the ways of the world.

In particular, the youth never knew fear.

He would listen to many people of the village say that when they passed by a graveyard they would shudder and pray for safety, but this only puzzled him. And when the town's elders would tell fantastical tales of haunting spirits, he would hear the listeners say, "That makes me shudder," but he never knew what they meant. This only caused the villagers to laugh and call him blockheaded.

One day, the youth decided to strike out into the world on his own, for he wanted to make his father proud by learning what it was to shudder. So the lad set out, saying, "If only I could shudder!"

Finally the boy wandered into a faraway kingdom. The king happened to be passing by when he heard the boy muttering, "O, I wish I could shudder."

The king stopped the boy and asked "What is it that you are saying?"

Said the boy, "I do so wish that I could shudder."

"What is this foolish chatter?" replied the king. "I will teach you such a thing, so come with me."

Now the king had promised his beautiful daughter in marriage to anyone who could stay in a haunted castle for three nights and then bring back the treasure therein. Those who had already tried never returned from the castle, but the king took the boy there and said, "Surely this will teach you."

The youth replied, "I will willingly spend three nights in this castle if it will teach me what I do not know." The king instructed the boy to only take three things with him into the castle. The boy thought and then asked for a fire, a turning lathe, and a cutting board with a knife. The king had these brought to the boy.

As night drew near, the lad entered the castle, made a fire in a large stone fireplace and sat patiently. Then, at the stroke of midnight, he heard a strange cry from a darkened corner, "Meow! Let us in from the cold night!"

"Why are you so stupid?" the boy replied. "If you are cold, sit in here by the fire." Then in leaped two black cats whose eyes glowed yellow. "Please, come sit with me, but first let me see your paws," said the youth. Upon seeing their sharp claws, the boy said, "My what sharp claws you have. I must cut them for you before you tear at the furniture." Thereupon he grabbed both cats, threw them down on the cutting board and said, "I have seen your sharp claws and I no longer wish to sit with you by the fire." Then he quickly struck them dead with the knife and threw them out the window into the moat.

But when he had done this, more black cats with yellow glowing eyes emerged from every corner of the room. He sat quietly watching them all for a while, but when the time was right, he grabbed the cutting knife and cried: "I have grown tired of you vermin. Be gone!" and began to cut them down. Some were killed and thrown into the moat and the rest disappeared into the dark shadows of the room.

When he was done, he sat once again by the fire, fanned the embers and warmed himself until he felt drowsy. He saw a bed in the corner and decided to lay down, but as he did, it began to move as though it had a life of its own. It danced and jumped and moved all over the castle. Instead of feeling fright, the boy laughed and urged the bed to go on running, only faster. But the bed grew weary and soon stood still. The boy said, "I enjoyed that tremendously! But now I must get some rest." So he laid down next to the fire and fell fast asleep.

The next morning, the king went up to the castle and saw the youth laying next to the fire. He thought the boy was dead, so he spoke aloud, saying, "What a pity!" But the boy then awakened and the king stood amazed that the youth had survived. "Have you learned to shudder yet?" the king asked.

"No. I wish someone would just tell me how it is done."

The second night the youth sat by the fire again. When midnight fell, he heard loud noises coming from the chimney. From that chimney fell half of a man. Soon after that, down came the other half. "Perhaps you need a fire," said the youth as he stoked the logs. When he turned back the two halves joined to form a hideous man, who now sat in the boy's chair.

Soon more dead men fell down. They brought nine dead men's legs and a skull and set them up and played at nine-pins with them. The youth, instead of feeling fear, said, "I should like to play at nine-pins too, but this ball is not quite round." He placed the skull into the lathe and turned it until it was round. "This should roll better," he said. With that, all the dead men vanished from the room as though they had never been there.

The next morning the king arrived to see if the boy had survived. He was surprised to find the youth in good spirits. "So you haven't learned to shudder then?" asked the king.

The boy said, "All I have learned is how to play at nine-pins. I wish someone would just tell me what it is to shudder."

The third night, as he sat by the fire, he said to himself, "I will never learn to shudder in this place!"

Just then an old man entered. He was taller than all the other spirits the youth had seen and he had a long, scraggly, white beard. "You fool!" said the man. "I shall be the one to teach you what it is to shudder, for soon I shall kill you."

"Please wait," said the youth. "If I am going to die, then I wish to have some say in it."

The fiend said, "I will soon grind you into dust."

To that, the boy replied, "If I were you, I would not talk like that. For, I am as strong as you are. Nay, I say that I am even stronger."

The fiend said, "We shall see. If you are stronger then I shall let you go." The old man led the youth down dark labyrinthine passages to a smith's forge, took an axe, and with one blow struck an anvil into the ground.

"I can do better than that," said the youth, who went to the anvil. The old man wanted to get a better look, so he drew near and his white beard hung down. The boy took the axe and with one blow, he split the anvil in two, catching the old man's beard in it. "Now it is you who will die," said the boy.

But the old man begged for mercy and told the boy that if he released him he would be rewarded with riches. The boy freed the axe and the old man led him to three chests of gold. When the clock struck midnight, the old man disappeared into the shadows and vanished from the castle.

The next morning, the king arrived early to see how the youth had fared. "You must have learned how to shudder by now," said the king.

"No," said the youth, "I saw an old man who showed me a room full of riches, but no one showed me how to shudder."

"Then," said the king, "my boy, you have saved the castle and you shall marry my daughter." Then the gold was brought up and the wedding was celebrated.[1]

Application of "The Boy Who Did Not Know How to Shudder"

In this story, the boy is full of the power to wonder. He chooses not to accept the culturally accepted, known reality of what should make him afraid. Initially, those around him call him blockheaded, stupid, and unable to learn anything. This symbolizes the culture's lack of flexibility. "There is only one way to be afraid," says society. Those who align with the power to wonder may similarly encounter protests from those around them who are held back by the restraints of knowledge.

But the youth of the story was saved by his own ability to wonder. Because his socially determined knowledge was limited, he operated from a self-determined knowledge—one that did not see ghosts as frightening.

The ghosts and goblins of the story symbolize the threshold of the cultural map that defined what it was people should be afraid of. These guardians were ineffective in the face of one accustomed to wondering and operating outside the boundaries of cultural map. Because the youth did not learn to be afraid of them, he moved beyond them effortlessly.

The result of this behavior was renewal. In other words, by refusing to accept the culturally accepted reality, the boy adopted an imaginative response that guided him through threatening situations and also won him the treasures, the maiden, and approval from the father-king figure, the symbol of the society.

Exercise: Making It Up

Think of a topic about which you know very little. Because you don't know much about this topic, make it up based on what information you do have. For example, if you know little about the Theory of Relativity, make it up. What would this theory mean if you were to have invented it? Who would it affect? What would it explain?

After you've finished doing this for a few minutes, take note of what happened to you internally. Did you become tense, bored, frustrated, or irritated that this was a waste of time? If so, try to infuse more wondering into your life.

Did you begin to feel as though this was fun and as though your consciousness was becoming supple? If so, then you are in natural alignment with wondering. Opening up to wondering is one way to begin to lighten up and become playful in our search for alternative solutions that apply to the challenges that face us.

Exercise: Unspoken Rules

Make a list of the unspoken rules that impact your behavior. Unspoken rules come from many sources such as your family or your culture. These rules are subtle and subjective guidelines that determine behavior. Discovering such rules is a trickier task than it first seems; there may be unspoken rules that operate completely unconsciously in your life. Here are some samples of unspoken rules: "We are a happy family." "Boys don't cry." "Don't show your emotions in public." "Everyone expects me to be nice." "Don't stare."

My unspoken rules:

1.

2.

3.

4.

5.

6.

7.

8.

9.

10.

Now, decide how each of the listed rules impacts your behavior. Which rules are worth keeping? Which rules need to be altered or discarded? Remember, the focus of widdershins work is to create internal movement—internal magic and transformation. One way this can be accomplished is by making unconscious material conscious.

Ritual of the Wand

In Neopagan spirituality, the wand is the magical tool associated with the powers of air and the east. It is traditionally constructed from a branch of oak or hazel wood and measures the length of your arm from your elbow to the tip of your index finger. On the wand you can inscribe sigils, signs, or emblems that evoke both the deosil power to know, and the widdershins power to wonder. You can use planetary sigils, or better yet, make them up! It is important that the imagery comes from your deep inner self, which is what guides all of your power.

This ritual will help you to merge with the power to wonder on the levels of body, mind, and spirit.

Items Needed:

- A magic wand.
- Dark Moon incense.
- Three Kings or some other self-igniting charcoal.
- An incense burner.

On a night of the dark or waning moon, gather the items listed. Face the east, light the charcoal in the incense burner, and sprinkle some of the incense on it.

Watch the smoke twist and move with the currents of air. See how freely it moves in time and space. It wanders here and there without any hesitation.

Body: To take in this power at the body level, begin to physically imitate the movement of the smoke. Hold the wand in a hand that is most comfortable, and with it trace the patterns of the smoke in the air. This will help you get a sense of the rhythm of the incense. Then, start at your toes and move all the way to the top of your head, moving each body part like the swirling incense.

Mind: After the dance you create on the physical level, sit down in front of the smoke, still facing the east. Place the wand in your lap. Now, allow your thoughts to wander like the smoke. Where does your mind go? Try not to guide it.

Spirit: Continue to sit facing the east. As you watch the smoldering incense, allow feelings to surface that correspond to the movement of the smoke. For example, if the smoke was creating a smooth, flowing pattern in the air, I would search for emotions that are similar to that smooth flowing pattern within me. It may be anger. It may be lightheartedness. What does the incense evoke in you? When you get a sensation of emotion, take note of where in your body you feel it. Pick up the wand, and with its tip, touch the place in your body where you felt the emotion, saying: *I welcome thee, powers of the widdershins east. I embrace the power to wonder.*

Whatever emotions emerged, allow them now to subside. If necessary, take a moment to ground and center yourself.

MEDITATION:

GAINING THE POWER TO WONDER

Close your eyes and take several deep breaths. Relax each part of the body, starting with the feet and moving all the way up to the top of your head. Let whatever tension you may be feeling flow into the ground, into the earth, where it is neutralized. Allow a blue mist to form around your feet and move all the way up your body until you are completely cocooned within the mist. Allow it to lift you up and take you on this journey of wonderment. You are being taken to a sacred place that your spirit has been once before. It is a place that allows your natural, child-like state of wondering to emerge.

[Partner: pause for a moment.]

The mist now sets you down, and as it does, it evaporates to reveal a new scene. You find yourself on the edge of a cliff looking out at the vast landscape below. The time is dawn, and you face the glowing eastern horizon. As the sun peeks little by little over the horizon, concentrate on thinking nothing at all. No words, no songs, no noise—simple stillness is called for here. Stay with this stillness as long as you can. Notice when you remain still that thoughts drift into your awareness. Simply observe them. Watch them go by and evaporate like clouds. Stay with the stillness. Notice how still and silent the landscape is below.

[Partner: pause for at least two minutes, but increase this pause by four minutes with each successive time the meditator tries this exercise.]

It is time to return now. The blue mist, once again, begins to form around your body, starting at your feet and moving upwards to completely envelope you. Allow the mist to bring you back to the place where your body rests comfortably. Once you are fully back, take time to answer the journaling questions.

JOURNALING

Describe the experience of remaining still from within.

What were some of the passing thoughts you had while attempting to keep your consciousness still?

Notes

1. Based on "The Man Who Did Not Know Fear," in Aleksandr Afanasev, *Russian Fairy Tales*, New York: Pantheon Books, 1973, pp. 325–327. Also based on translations of "The Youth Who Went Forth to Learn What Fear Was," by Marian Edwards and Edgar Taylor, in Jacob and Wilhelm Grimm, *Fairy Tales*, New York: Alfred A. Knopf, Inc., 1992, pp. 348–359.

Chapter 9

The Power to Resonate

The names *Goddess*, *God*, and *deity* are all words that refer to something that cannot really be captured by words. This is because words themselves are limitations. When we apply words to describe the dimension of deity, they fall short and feel mechanical. Language cannot adequately describe a dimension that transcends all categories of thought. Trying to describe deity in words is like trying to do the same with colors or music.

Mystics and shamans around the world symbolize deity as "the void," rather than trying to capture it with concrete words. The void is a space of silence, which is the power of the north in the deosil spiral of traditional Wicca.

Although this dimension is difficult to put into human words, it is relatively accessible to human experience. Accessing deity through experience is the widdershins power of the north: the power to resonate.

When you resonate, the void fills with the intelligible presence of deity. The power to resonate then means the power to "draw down the

Gods", as the Witches say, into your being. Through the process of drawing down the Gods, you become a channel for divine presence.

When you draw down the pure power of deity into human consciousness, it is like light passing through a prism. It splits into an infinite number of rays, or aspects, as they are called in magical work. Your body, mind, and spirit become like a transmitter for one aspect or another of deity through the magical practice of resonance.

For example, on nights of the full moon, when a Wiccan spiritual community gathers to create magic, a priestess is selected to draw down the Moon, which means she invokes the Goddess' presence into their magic circle through her own consciousness. To achieve this, the priestess goes into a trance, through either ecstatic dance or meditation, and surrenders her body, mind, and spirit to the Goddess. She then becomes a direct conduit of deity power and may "speak with her tongue," and "touch with her hands," as one Witch invocation says. Once the priestess is divinely possessed, she carries the Goddess' powers.

There is a similar practice for male coven members, which is called drawing down the Sun, or drawing down the God. Men channel the God at Wiccan fire festivals, such as at the equinoxes or solstices.

Now it is your turn to fill the void and directly link to the experience of deity. Each of the widdershins powers in turn has led you to the power of resonance. In the west, you learned to ground and center your consciousness, which is the first step in moving into your inward life. In the south, you learned to surrender, relax, or release the body and the mind. In the east, you practiced opening your consciousness to wandering beyond the limits of what is known. And in this final power, your body, mind, and spirit are purposely unobstructed in a sacred and magical setting, in order to align with the powers of the Gods.

Every culture of the world that has ever included magic in its belief system, has practiced some form of divine possession or resonance.[1] In Ariège, France, there are cave paintings that may well indicate an understanding of resonance from as long as 15,000 years ago. The cave wall is covered with sacred images, and one in particular stands out. It is that of a half man, half animal creature that anthropologists call the "Sorcerer Les Trois Frères." The figure stands on two human feet, but he has the tail and antlers of a deer, the eyes of an owl, and the genitalia are placed like a feline's.

This cave image dates back to the Upper Paleolithic period in Europe,[2] and some experts consider this and other similar images in caves throughout Europe (such as those depicting dancing bison-men), to be the oldest representations of shamanic activity.[3] Anthropologists and folklorists argue over whether these figures represent either shamans or deities, but in the moment of resonance, when the shaman is possessed by the deity, there is no difference between the two.

The ancients Egyptians also knew the power of resonance as well, and spoke of it in their *Book of the Dead* as a necessary power for those journeying through the Underworld. The person on such a journey was to identify completely with the Gods by affirming:

> *My hair is the hair of Nu. My face is the face of the Disk. My eyes are the eyes of Hathor. My ears are the ears of Apuat. My nose is the nose of Khenti-khas. My lips are the lips of Anpu.... There is no member of my body that is not the member of some God. The God Thoth shields my body altogether, and I am Re day by day....[4]*

Mythologizing each part of the body so that it took on sacred meaning was an effective way of aligning their consciousness with the divine.

Another well-documented account of the practice of resonance occurs in ancient Greece. The Priestesses of the Oracle at Delphi spoke with the voice and authority of the Goddess, for once in trance they resonated with Her power.

In contemporary Bushman societies, the state of resonance comes through the trance dance called Ntum. In this dance, the women of the village sit in a circle and beat their thighs like drums. The men dance on the outside of the circle to the rhythm that the women create. During the dance, some of the men "transform" into the tribal Gods in an ecstatic state[5]—a state of greatly heightened internal and external awareness.[6]

The practice of resonance is relatively easy for Neopagan folk to assimilate into their magical work, because their world view allows for direct interaction with the Gods. The earth, the circling planets, the stars, and galaxies comprise the bodies of the Goddess and the God. Earth-centered spirituality does not place deity away from humanity. It places humanity at the center of divinity. Witches and shamans know that they are, themselves, both the creation and that which creates.

Binnorie

Once upon a time a king had two daughters who lived in a bower near the mill-dams of Binnorie. The two daughters were lovely to behold. So lovely was the eldest that Sir William came wooing her and won her love. But then, after a time, he looked upon the younger sister, with her golden hair and long, elegant hands, and his love went out to her until he no longer loved the elder one. The elder sister became so jealous and filled with hate for her younger sister that she finally plotted to do away with her.

One day, the eldest implored her sister to accompany her to watch the boats coming in at the mill stream of Binnorie. The youngest, who had no idea of her sister's jealousy, agreed. So together they went hand in hand. They came to the river's bank and the younger sister got up on a rock to get a good view of the boats beaching, when the eldest came from behind her and pushed her into the rushing mill stream.

"O sister, reach me your hand!" cried the younger sister as she floated away, "and I shall give you half of all that I own."

The elder sister replied, "No sister, I shall not reach you a hand. Shame on me if I help the one that has come 'twixt me and my own love's heart."

And the young princess floated down the mill stream, sometimes swimming, sometimes sinking, until she came near the miller's dam. Now, the miller's daughter was cooking that day, and she needed water for her bread. As she went to draw the water, she spotted something floating towards the mill-dam. "Father, father," she cried, "something white is coming downstream. Perhaps it is a bonny swan."

Her father hastened to the dam only to discover the princess, fair and beautiful, who now laid dead on the shore. "O woe!" cried the miller's daughter, "the swan has drowned!" So, together, they laid the princess on the river's bank.

As she lay there, a famous harper, who was also a wise man, passed by the mill-dam of Binnorie and saw the lovely princess' face. Though he had traveled on far away, he never forgot that face, and after many days he returned to the mill-dam of Binnorie. But by that time, all he could find of her were her bones and her golden hair. So he made a harp of her breast bone, used her hair for harp strings and the bones of her long slender hands for the harp pins. He then traveled up the hill from the mill-dam to the castle of the king, her father.

That night, the court was assembled to hear the great harper play. The elder daughter was present in the assembly, and she stood alongside her lover, Sir William. The harper set the harp he had just made down on a stone in the hall. Then he sat down to sing with his old harp, when presently, the harp on the stone began to sing by itself in a low, clear tone. All in the assembly were hushed by the enchanting music.

O yonder sits my father, the king,
Binnorie, O Binnorie;
And yonder sits my mother, the queen;
By the bonnie mill-dams of Binnorie.

And yonder sits my brother, Hugh,
Binnorie, O Binnorie;
And by him, William, false and true;
By the bonnie mill-dams of Binnorie.

They all wondered what the song could mean, and the harper told them how he had seen the princess lying drowned near the mill-dams of Binnorie and how after many days he made this harp with her fingers, hair, and breast bone. Just then, the harp sang again:

And yonder sits my sister who drowned me
By the bonnie mill-dams of Binnorie.

Then the harp stood silent, but all assembled knew what had happened. The older sister was so filled with shame that she left the kingdom, never to return again.[7]

APPLICATION OF "BINNORIE"

The crucial moment, that of magical transformation in the tale of Binnorie, occurs when the young princess is killed. She leaves her physical form behind, which is the first step toward resonance. Resonance propels you beyond the physical and toward the spiritual so that you can become like the princess in her second phase, an instrument of the

Gods. The symbol of the princess-as-harp represents a transformation from the physical realm to the spiritual. The young princess became a harp, an instrument of resonance, and she spoke with the voice of truth—that of the Gods—which is what happens to you when you draw down the Gods into your being. No longer are you a human being in that instance. You lose your physical self and become like the princess—immortal.

Pentacle Meditation

The pentacle is the magical tool of the north, of earth, in traditional Wicca. The pentacle is a disk usually made of wood, metal, or clay on which is inscribed a five-pointed star made of intersecting lines. For this exercise, you can draw your own pentacle on a sheet of blank parchment paper if you do not own the traditional tool. Four of the five points of the pentacle correspond to the four earthly elements. The fifth point of the pentacle represents spirit, the final element that contains all of the other four.

In traditional Wicca, the pentacle is typically depicted with the apex of spirit on top. The pentagram drawn this way is a symbol for the idea that matter has its origins in spirit. It means the physical plane is a manifestation or emanation of the spiritual. Spirit descends or flows into matter in this symbol. Through this exercise, you will begin to allow the flow of spirit into the physical realm through your own body.

To begin, stand facing the north, with your feet spread apart. Place the pentacle on the ground before you, close your eyes, and center yourself in time and place. Then, imagine that from your feet grow roots that extend deep into the earth. Feel the still, cool, moist planet beneath you. Outstretch your arms to your sides so that they are level with your shoulders, palms facing out, toward the north.[8] Feel the magnetic pull of the north that tugs on your hands.

Beneath the silence of the earth, you feel a low vibration. It may feel weak at first, but the longer you stay with it, the stronger it becomes. As you stay with this, notice that your body begins to vibrate in unison with the earth. Now use your voice to generate a sound that is an extension of this deep vibration. Resonate. Fill the silence with the sound of the earth, for you are her voice. Sustain this for as long as you can. Then allow the sound to subside, to fade back into the silence from which it came.

See how you yourself are the five points of the pentacle and that you contain all. Know that you are the five senses of the earth. You speak, feel, taste, smell, and touch for the earth. You are the resonance of the earth. Now say:

> Blessed be my hands. Blessed be my eyes.
> Blessed be my tongue. Blessed be my nose.
> Blessed be my ears. For I touch, see, taste, smell,
> And hear the presence of the gods.
> They are within and without!
> I welcome thee, powers of the widdershins north.
> I embrace the power to resonate!

RESONANCE RITUAL

Most Witches practice some form of drawing down the Gods in their ceremonies. Typically they do this magical work on nights of the full moon. However, resonance is a dark moon power that can be done at any time. Remember, the phase of the moon is simply a symbol indicating what should be going on inside each of us. The magic of resonance can happen at any moon or sun tide with a bit of practice.

When you channel the Gods, they lend you their power. Most often, this power lingers far after the ritual. This is power that you may put to good use.

It is also important to know that resonance should be practiced solely within a sacred space—a magic circle. The circle provides a protection for your body as you allow the Gods to channel through you, as well as a focus—like a lens—for specifically touching the realm of deity. First of all, the magic circle is like a protective layer that shields your body from magical or spiritual attack while you channel. This is important, because through this work you temporarily displace your spirit from your body to make room for deity.

Also, if resonance is practiced outside of a sacred space, you can easily tap into entities that are not the Goddess or God. Some people purposely attempt to tap into realms other than that of deity, but I neither recommend it nor practice it. Information you may receive from a drifting discarnate spirit is highly suspect. As one Wiccan priestess used to say, "Just because you're dead doesn't mean you're smart." Staying within the magic circle while you resonate assures you of a safe and sacred experience.

Moon Phase: any.

Purpose: to gain the powers of the Gods.

Items Needed:

- A pentacle.
- Delphi incense.[9]
- Delphi oil.[10]
- An incense burner.
- Your usual tools for casting a circle.

Begin casting a circle. If you are in a waxing moon cycle, cast a deosil circle; if in a waning moon cycle, cast a widdershins circle.[11]

Take the mixture of salt and water you used to cast your circle and dab a bit of it on the soles of your feet. Then dab a bit on the top of your head and say:

All that is between earth and water belongs to the Mighty Ones.

Light the Delphi incense in the incense burner and place it on the floor. Hold one foot at a time over the smoke, then lift the incense burner and fan some smoke across the top of your head, saying:

All that is between fire and air belongs to the Mighty Ones.

Set the incense back on the altar. Next, anoint the soles of your feet with Delphi oil. As you do this say:

Blessed be my feet, for my journey has brought me in a sacred way.

Anoint the center of energy at the top of your head with the oil to open this psychic center. Then say:

All that is between thee is the mighty Ones.

Stand facing the north with your feet apart in the magic circle's center and place the pentagram beneath you. Next you will begin the meditation below to invoke the Gods. Some people find standing too distracting for this work. If this is the case for you, sit facing north with your legs crossed and your back straight. Place the pentagram in front of you. For best results, have a magical partner read the guided imagery to come, or have it tape-recorded prior to the working.

DRAWING DOWN THE GODS

Close your eyes and take several deep, slow breaths. Focus on exhaling as you continue to breathe deeply. Imagine that you are becoming the outgoing breath. The breathing, the breather and the breath are one.

Imagine that a mist of indiscernible color begins to form around your feet. It slowly spirals counterclockwise and upward around your legs, thighs, hips, stomach, chest, arms, shoulders, neck, and head. It has now completely enveloped you.

Within the swirling mist, there is a doorway. Go to it. When you get there, step through the doorway. Once you do that, the scene immediately changes. You now find that you are standing before your own body, which you see is enshrouded in mist. Continue to breathe deeply and slowly.

[Partner: pause for a moment.]

Imagine that you pick up the pentacle and hold it over your mist-covered body's head. As soon as you do this, a bright ray of light beams down through the body. This is the power of the Gods filling you. Listen closely to whatever words or sounds that may come from your mist-covered body, for these are the words of the Goddess or the God.

Whatever words you hear, utter them aloud—whether or not there are other folks attending your circle. If you wish, you may simply listen to and remember the words of the Gods. I perfer to utter their words aloud because though it may feel contrived at first, there will come a point when the words come without your assistance. That is the point at which you have completely melded with the Gods. In this practice, some people never actually hear words; instead they sense what is being said. Sometimes the Gods will ask questions of you directly. Other times they may have messages, questions, or comments for individuals outside of the magic circle. Whatever may come of the rite, be as pure of a channel as possible.

[Partner: pause while priest/ess channels. If the priest/ess pauses for a very long time, the message may possibly be complete. If so, continue reading.]

Each Goddess or God carries an aspect of power. Take a moment to sense what powers are being lent to you. When the message from the Goddess or God is complete, the shaft of light will withdraw from the mist-covered body. When that happens, you are immediately transported to the doorway leading into the mist. Step through the door, and soon the mist carries you back to the room, back to the place where your body rests comfortably. After you are set back down into your body, take a moment to open your eyes, stretch, then ground yourself again in time and place.

The rite is complete. Close your circle as usual.

Alternate Trance Induction: Ecstatic Dance

Another traditional, shamanic method to induce resonance is through "ecstatic dance." This is a dynamic method of drawing down the Gods, and is just as effective as using guided imagery. The choice between ecstatic dance and meditation is purely a matter of personal taste.

Just as in the meditation, the idea behind this work is to displace the critical faculties so that deity can channel through you unimpeded.

◑ **Needed:** a drummer or a drumming tape.

To begin, follow the previous steps of casting the circle and anointing yourself. Once that has been done, place your pentacle on the ground in front of you as you face the north.

Turn on the drumming tape or have your magical partner begin drumming.

Listen to the beat and allow the rhythm to sweep over you. Allow each beat and each pause within the rhythm to suggest a movement to various parts of your body. Allow this to be random. In one set of beats, you may find your knees lifting and turning; in another set, you may begin to roll your head; in another, you may extend your arms. Work with this for few minutes.

Next, begin to combine the body movements. Allow each isolated hip movement and foot stomp (or whatever it is your body is doing) to unite. Let each part build into a whole. Don't try to make sense of it. Don't try to edit. Don't worry about how it looks to others.

Continue this until you reach the point where you feel like you are no longer within your body. To facilitate this, imagine that you are within the circle, merely watching your body dance. When you do this, imagine that a shaft of brilliant white light beams through your body as it dances.

Once that happens, the dance may do one of two things: it may become wilder, or it may slow down. If it gets even wilder, do not expect that you will be able to speak the words of the Gods. Listen to them and remember them for later. If you see your body beginning to slow down, listen to the words of the Gods and then give them voice.

At some point, the shaft of light will disappear. When that happens, typically you will find that your body is becoming limp. Allow yourself time to sit or lay down after this working. Be certain that you ground yourself after the dance.

JOURNALING

Which aspect of deity did I channel? (Goddess, God, names?)

What was the message of the Gods? How clear was the message?

What will make the next resonance ritual more effective?

With what powers or abilities was I imbued?

Notes

1. James G. Frazer, *The Golden Bough*, New York: Avenel Books, 1981 (originally published 1890), p. 32.

2. For more information see, e.g., Marija Gimbutas, *The Language of the Goddess*, New York: Harper-Collins, 1989, pp. 175–183.

3. Margaret Murray, *The God of the Witches*, New York: Oxford University Press, 1970 pp. 23, 24, 30.

4. Based on translations by E.A.W. Budge, *The Book of the Dead, the Papyrus of Ani, Scribe and Treasurer of the Temples of Egypt*, about B.C.E. 1450. See, e.g. Joseph Campbell, *The Hero With A Thousand Faces*, New Jersey: Princeton University Press, 1973, p. 371.

5. Joseph Campbell, Betty Sue Flowers (ed.), *The Power of Myth*, New York: Doubleday, p. 87.

6. Timothy Roderick, *The Once Unknown Familiar*, St. Paul: Llewellyn Publications, 1994, p. 64.

7. Based on translations of the tale of Binnorie. Joseph Jacobs, *English Folk and Fairy Tales*, (3rd edition, revised) New York: G. P. Putnam's Sons, (n.d.), pp. 43–47.

8. In traditional Wicca, this body posture is called the "pentacle position."

9. See Appendix B for recipe.

10. See Appendix B for recipe.

11. See Appendix A for circle casting methods.

Part III

Spells:
Dark Moon Crafts

Chapter 10

The Ways of Dark Moon Magic

The Sage speaks:

I have grown old. Death speaks to my brittle bones, calling to me. My child in the Gods, the time has come for me to pass the final few secrets of my crafts on to you. Your journey to this point was far, but now the true voices of your guidance, those of the Old Ones, speak only of you. They bespeak the season of your power, which comes to term under the last days of the darkened moon. Courage is yours, as you have passed shadow's initiation. Strength is yours, as you have learned to harmonize with dark-ness. And now, my wise one, you stand between darkness and reemergence into light. You stand on the edge of enchantment, between worlds known and unknown.

It is here in your age of power that I give you my dark moon crafts. These are the magics of transition, completion, discovery, mystery, and return. Fulfill your destiny to resonate with the spiraling cycle of life, from birth and death through rebirth, by spiraling inward.

Be ever mindful that balance is key to mastery of dark moon magics, as it is with the light. Spiraling inward to the dark, to inner depths, is especially beneficial when you spiral back out into action, into the light—and the reverse of that holds true as well.

I say to you, look here: each moon cycle, both light and dark, calls for a transformation of your inner vision to make an ally of these magical tides. This is a simple matter, really. The waxing moon gains light; work magic in the direction of increase at this tide. The waning moon dies to light; work magic in the direction of decrease at this tide. Learn to flow with the moon, and the moon will yield Her bounty.

Che Dark Moon Deicies

The unconscious mind governs the magic of the moon in any of its phases, as we have explored earlier, and the unconscious speaks in symbol language. The Goddesses and Gods known by various names and guises throughout all time, in every culture, are the symbols that are universal, the archetypes of dark moon magic. It is beneficial, then, for us to become familiar with these deities and archetypal powers before practicing the dark moon magic of the European shamans and Witches.

At the risk of being overly simplistic, the Goddess is the symbol of the divine feminine principle in traditional European lore, an archetypal construct that provides us with a rich and multi-layered symbol system. The subtleties of Goddess energies are understood with relative ease by their phases of life: Maidens, Mothers, and Crones. These three represent the universal life stages of womanhood: youth, maturity, and old age.

The divine male principle, the Gods, is also divided into three categories that likewise correspond to men's life experience through youth, maturity, and, of course, old age. These three faces of the God are, respectively, Inseminator, Provider, and Sage.

In dark moon magic, the presiding deities are the Crone and the Sage. Both deities symbolize advancing age and the wisdom that accrues with the passage of time. The Crone is the image of woman beyond child-bearing years, and similarly, the Sage represents men who have moved from a focus on their life of outward movement and achievement to a focus on their inner wisdom.

The following charts illustrate the powers associated with Crone and Sage magic. These are the energies that govern the enchantments in the Grimoire to follow.

Female Archetype:	Maiden	Mother	Crone
Male Archetype:	Inseminator	Provider	Sage

Moon Phase:	Waxing	Full	Waning
Energies associated:	commencement	accomplishment	completion
	beginning	development	ending
	newness	expansion	culmination
	initiation	attainment	dissolution
	birth	growth	death
	action	fulfillment	introspection
	inception	achievement	return
	planting	fruition	reaping
	sprouting	flowering	harvesting
	youth	maturity	old age
	ingenuity	prosperity	decay
	novelty	progress	tradition
	inspiration	realization	wisdom
	movement	presence	vision

Crone Goddesses: Hecate, Medusa, Kali, Oya, Cerridwen, Cybelle, Durga, Hella, Artimis, Sekhmet, Frau Holle, Persephone, Sheela-na-gig.

Sage Gods: Thor, Shiva, Zeus, Neptune, Cernunnos, Osiris, Ra, Set, Thanatos, Wotan, Odin, Mithra, Hades, Prometheus, Tethra, Thoth.

The Widdershins Grimoire

Dark Moon Divinations: The Magic Mirror

The magic mirror is a scrying[1] device that contemporary Witches utilize to see mystical visions of the past, present, or future. Legends, myths, and fairy tales are replete with examples of the power associated with this tool, which attests to its antiquity. For example, in the tale of Snowdrop, the heroine's stepmother would gaze into a "fairy looking glass" and chant:

> Tell me glass, tell me true!
> Of all the ladies in the land,
> Who is the fairest, tell me, who?[2]

And, of course, the mirror would respond in kind. Because these tales refer to this magical tool, the mirror has become itself an archetype. It is symbolic of the gift of prophecy, of vision. It is the symbol of the experience of mystery and discovery, of looking into our own spirit to find what powers dwell there.

The use of a mirror as a tool of magical vision reverberates within the unconscious and immediately engages us in the mystery of its workings. However, there is very little mystery involved with the makings of a magic mirror. It is not only easy to make, but with a little practice, you can use it to open your consciousness to new levels of insight and power.

Constructing Your Magic Mirror

Items Needed:

- ◑ A photo frame with a removable back and removable glass, at least large enough for an 8" x 10" insert.[3]

- ◑ Black, high-gloss paint (not the aerosol spray variety).

- ◑ The following dried and powdered herbs: hyssop, dragon's blood reed (pre-powdered), orris root (pre-powdered), anise seed, and any variety of dried moss.

- ◑ A disposable mixing container (such as a paint can).

- ◑ A paintbrush.

Collect the items listed above during a waning moon cycle. In a mortar or some other smooth vessel, crush the herbs into a powder and then scoop them together into a heap. These herbs all have properties that enhance psychic development. Take out the jar of black paint and pour a portion of it into the disposable mixing dish. Slowly stir small portions of the herb mixture into the paint until you have a thick, tar-like substance.

While you are adding in the herbs, begin to raise power by chanting the following:

> Vision of night,
> By the moon's dark light,
> Enter my art!
> All evil depart!

To raise power, start chanting the spell slowly and softly. Gradually, increase your volume, pitch, and speed. As you do this, imagine rays of moonlight beaming down into your mixture. Feel the power brimming inside of you, and once you feel filled with energy, channel it into the paint-herb mixture.

Next, take your photo frame, open the back, and remove the glass. Begin brushing the glass with the herb-paint mixture. Paint as evenly as possible using long, smooth strokes. Be certain to cover only one side of the glass entirely—leave no unpainted areas anywhere on that one surface! Wait for the paint to dry and then replace the glass into the frame, so that the shiny glass part shows through the frame. This glass is the scrying surface into which you will peer for visions.

Consecrating and Empowering the Magic Mirror

Items Needed:

- Completed magic mirror.
- A black veil or any other black cloth.
- Dark Moon incense.[4]
- A dish of salt and a dish of water.
- A purple candle, inscribed with the symbol of the waning moon (see illustration at right).
- Four white votive candles (tea lights).
- Wisdom oil.[5]

Do this magical working within your dark moon circle to properly consecrate the mirror.[6] Once the circle is cast, place the mirror on your altar and cover this with the veil or black cloth. Place the purple candle behind the mirror and the four votive candles around it at each of the four cardinal directions, east, south, west, and north. Each of these votives should be no more than five inches from the mirror.

Light each of the candles beginning in the west and ending in the north. As you light the west candle, say:

> The west's only daughter,
> The moon's flowing heart,
> By fish, fin, and water
> Intuition impart!

Light the southern-most candle, saying as you light it:

> Powers of fire
> Flicker and flair
> Through the mirror inspire
> Your prophecies rare.

Light the east candle, saying:

> The power of air
> This mirror doth wield
> It blows to this priest(ess)
> Dark visions revealed!

Light the northern-most candle, saying:

> **Powers of earth**
> **In midnight's black hour,**
> **The mirror gives birth**
> **To your silent power.**

Next, ignite the Dark Moon incense by sprinkling a bit of it over a charcoal briquette. Light the purple candle and then remove the veil from the mirror. Consecrate the mirror with water and salt, touching a bit of each to the scrying surface. Pass the mirror's scrying surface over the smoldering incense and also over the purple candle's flame.

Lay the mirror flat on the altar and hold your hands over the scrying surface. Draw down the power of the dark moon through your third eye, the psychic center that rests in the center of your brow, about a quarter-inch above where your nose meets your brow. To do this, imagine that you draw the energy of the moon in along with your breath, and begin to channel that energy through your hands into the mirror.

Continue this for a few minutes, or until you feel the mirror is fully charged. Still holding your hands over the mirror's surface, blow out the east candle, saying:

> **The power to wonder!**

Blow out the southern candle, saying:

> **The power to surrender!**

Blow out the west candle, saying:

> **The power to accept!**

Finally, blow out the northern candle, saying:

> **The power to resonate!**

Lastly, anoint the four corners of the mirror's frame with wisdom oil, and then anoint the center of the mirror's scrying surface. While doing so, recite the following chant:

> **Visions of the darkened mother**
> **And dread horned lord,**[7]
> **Let fall the deep purple veil**
> **Of the priestess and priest!**
> **Reveal to me thine ecstacy!**

Some people even "lock" the powers of the mirror to their use alone by charging it with a secret, magic word. To do this, at the time that you anoint the mirror's center, keep your fingers on the mirror's surface and say your magic word three times. Between each utterance of the word, remove your hands from the mirror's center and breathe *through* the spot. Allow your psychic energy to mingle with the mirror's.

Now your mirror is properly charged and ready for use.

USING THE MAGIC MIRROR

With your magic mirror properly charged and consecrated, you will want to seek its visions at the time of the waning or dark moon. To properly induce magic mirror visions, it is best to place a votive candle behind the mirror, so that you cannot see both the mirror and the flame simultaneously. You can seek the magic mirror's visions outside of the construct of your magic circle, but for the clearest visions or for visions inspired only by the divine, it is advisable to work within the magic circle.

When you are ready, hold your hands over the surface of the mirror and whisper your magic word three times. Rest your hands on the table and gaze steadily into the mirror's blackness. Don't look at the surface, but *through* the surface. Allow your mind to be still, or if you have a specific intention or question you'd like addressed, fix your thoughts on that while gazing. Images, colors, and sometimes even sounds will soon begin to reveal themselves.

If this method fails to produce effective results, try extinguishing the candle and tenting your veil over both you and the mirror. Gaze into the mirror and expect visions to emerge.

Some readers will easily adapt to this divinatory method; others will require more practice before they attain results. It took one man in my coven months before he was able to see anything in the magic mirror.

The Wheel of Fate

The Wheel of Fate is a technique used to discover the influences of past lives on your present life. During the dark moon, karma is an important subject to explore. Through careful contemplation, you can discover its effects and can alter your present behaviors and attitudes that contribute to perpetuate the karmic cycle. In other words, when you know what actions stimulate karmic results, you can begin to alter that karma by altering your actions.

It is difficult to determine whether or not a given circumstance in our lives is the result of past life karma. However, good indicators of this are:

- Patterns that continually repeat (for example, always being cheated by others or always winning some type of game).

- A situation that manifests, yet does not appear to be the consequence of any direct action (for example, being hit by a car, despite your prudent driving record, or winning the lottery).

To divine the nature of the karma involved, use the following method. On a large cloth approximately 2' x 2,' paint the diagram shown at the top of page 152.

Select the deck of tarot cards that feels the most comfortable to you. Use the listing below to decide which area of your life is most affected by karma. For each grouping of life categories, there is a representative zodiacal glyph or symbol. Whichever category most represents your area of life effected by karma, take note of the corresponding glyph.

♈ (Aries)—Beginnings, appearances, outlook on life, physical body, personality.

♉ (Taurus)—Values, freedom, money, inner resources, material resources, earning ability, possessions.

♊ (Gemini)—Travel, communication, conscious mind processes, early education, intelligence, brothers and sisters.

♋ (Cancer)—Home, endings, property, foundations, latter part of life.

♌ (Leo)—Sports, children, creativity, love that you give, love affairs, speculations, romance.

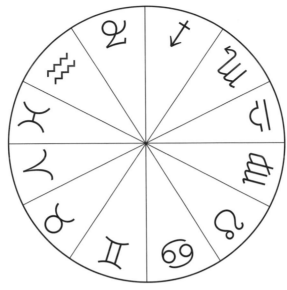

The Wheel of Fate

℞ (Virgo)—Health, habits, unconscious mind, service given, work, jobs, pets.

♎ (Libra)—Marriage, partners, public relations, art, entertainment, enemies, others as they relate to you.

♏ (Scorpio)—Sex, taxes, death, your partner's resources or resources that you've amassed in a partnership, inheritance, regeneration.

♐ (Sagittarius)—Religion, philosophy, spiritual activity, traveling long distances, laws, in-laws.

♑ (Capricorn)—Reputation, career, authorities, status, ego, politics.

♒ (Aquarius)—Goals, friends, hopes, wishes, circumstances beyond one's control, love received.

♓ (Pisces)—Limitations, frustrations, hidden strengths, unconscious processes.

Next, place the cloth on a flat horizontal surface with the painted wheel in front of you, so that Aries (♈) is the house or area of interest on the direct west of you (or on your left side).

Next, relax your body and journey within to ask your wisdom self for enlightenment regarding the karmic influences in your life. Once you have requested assistance and aligned with your wisdom, shuffle the tarot deck and fan the cards out on a table top. With your eyes closed and while concentrating on discovering past life influences in your particular area of interest, run your hands along the cards and select two of them. Place these cards down on the Wheel of Fate cloth, placing them nearby the sign of your house of interest like this:

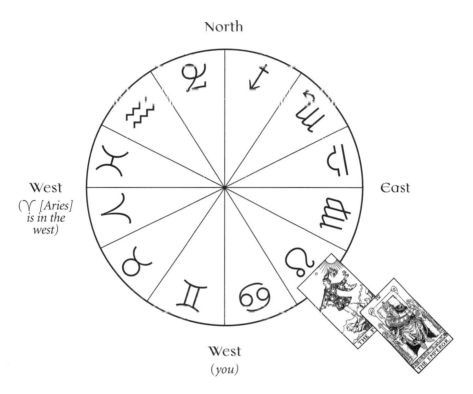

The first card laying next to the sign or glyph will represent the current influences in this area. The second card will illustrate a past life influence that is affecting this house of interests. If you have little or no experience in interpreting the tarot, consult a basic book, such as Eden Grey's *Tarot Revealed,* Angelus Arrian's *The Tarot Handbook,* or Zerner & Farber's *The Enchanted Tarot.*

It is entirely possible that there may be more than one past life influence impacting the course of your life. You can consult the oracle again to determine what current past-life influences are involved in any situation.

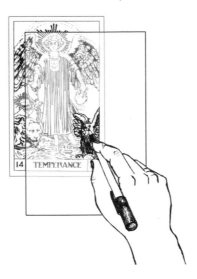

A Spell Co Resolve Karmic Debc

Use this technique once you've created your magic mirror and have completed the Wheel of Fate divination to discover a karmic effect from a past life. Gather the following items once you have the card that represents the karmic debt from a past life:

- Your magic mirror.
- A sheet of onion skin parchment paper or tracing paper (or any other paper that allows you to see an image through it).
- 1 oz. of the following herbs, combined, dried, and powdered: fern, black cohosh, hyssop, and powdered oak wood.[8]
- A red-inked pen.

Moon Phase: Waning/3rd quarter.

Purpose: to resolve past-life influences.

Create sacred space by constructing a dark moon circle. Once the circle is up, take the tarot card representing your karmic debt and place it before you. Stare at the image for a while and allow it to become impressed upon your inner eye, so that when you close your eyes, you can still see the card and all its detail clearly. Begin to softly repeat the following chant:

To bane! To bane!
The blackened gate,
Reveal the image
Of my fate.

As you do this you will notice that at least one specific image from the card will become prominent in your psychic vision. For instance, the eyes of a character in the illustration might become prominent, or a cluster of grapes might come to the fore.

When this happens, stop chanting and consult your inner Crone or Sage to discover the meaning of the image. To do this, allow stillness to overcome you, and listen for the inner voice of the Crone or Sage to come forward. What does the Crone or Sage say? What is this image in relation to your karmic tie? Once you know this, ask what must be done to resolve the karmic debt. What does the voice of your inner wisdom tell you?

After your images and inner wisdom have revealed themselves, cover the tarot card with the onion skin or other translucent paper. Use the red-inked pen to trace the images from the card that were prominent in the vision. Draw an invoking earth pentagram around the traced images and a circle around the pentagram, so it looks something like the diagram below.

At the four quarters of the encircled pentagram, on the outside perimeter, draw four Saturn[9] sigils. It will now look like this:

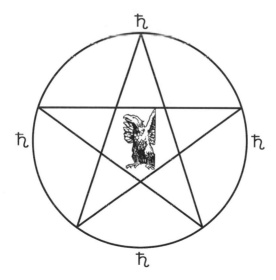

Cut out this talisman, so that the paper is in the shape of a square. Put a small quantity of the herb mixture in the center of the talisman and twist the whole thing closed. Set this bundle aside for a moment. Next, take the same tarot card and place it face down on the magic mirror and sprinkle some herbs on this as well.

Then place the twisted-up talisman-herb bundle into a burning vessel and light the bundle on fire, allowing it to burn completely. As it burns, imagine the karmic forces resolving themselves while chanting:

> The deed has done! to bane! begone!
> The Crone (Sage)[10] has reaped her (his) bitter corn.
> And while her (his) scythe is sheathed
> The sun's rays drift in wakened morn
> To Saturn's ways forever done! To bane! Begone!
> To bane! Begone!

The ceremonial portion of your spell is now completed. Your next step is to take whatever actions are necessary to resolve the karmic tie.

The Black Bowl

The black bowl has a similar function to the magic mirror, but its design can add new aspects to your divinatory work. The black bowl uses water as its scrying surface and water is a natural conduit of psychic visions. Since both the Mirror and the bowl accomplish the same magical ends, it is really a matter of personal taste that will determine which method best suits you.

Witches consult the black bowl during the dark of the moon, which is, of course, the lunar tide that draws us inward, where our psychic abilities lie. The black bowl differs from the Magic Mirror in that it is used for divination and generally not for magic. The reason for this is that the black bowl uses water, which has a changeable quality. For most magical operations, particularly for magic that requests a manifestation, it is best to use a more solid, earthy conduit. Water has the ability to transform a negative situation into an entirely positive one when used magically. However, because the basic nature of the element is changeability, it is difficult to predict the outcome of consciously directing energy through the black bowl's divining water.

CONSTRUCTING YOUR BLACK BOWL

Moon Phase: 4th quarter.

Purpose: constructing and consecrating a black bowl for divination.

Items Needed:

- ◑ A large, deep bowl. This bowl can be any dark color, but black is preferable.

- ◑ If you want the bowl to be black, get high-gloss enamel black paint. Also you may want enamel paints to decorate the outside of the bowl with sigils. Select whatever colors speak to your unconscious. Some traditional colors used in decorating the black bowl include metallic silver, gold, bronze, white or red.

The bowl does not have to be black, but a solid, dark color of some sort is preferable. Or simply blacken the inside of any bowl that you like, up to the outer lip. Use the silver and white paints to add runes, lunar glyphs, magical names, God or Goddess sigils, or anything that makes the bowl a tool—something which is elevated from the ranks of a mundane, household object.

To further decorate the black bowl, you could even glue cowrie shells on the outside, in deference to the Goddess, and as a connection to the element of water, which is traditionally a female element. Try adhering some of these objects:

coins	pieces of silver	sacred stones
beads	leather thongs	feathers
pentagrams	Goddess images	dried herbs
mirror pieces	dried flowers	chips of colored glass

With a bit of imagination, a myriad of possibilities will emerge.

CONSECRATING THE BLACK BOWL

Once you've designed and constructed your black bowl, it is time to attune it to *divine* energies. *Divination* is a word that incorporates the term divine, indicating communication with the Gods. Instead of opening consciousness to the divine, often people will open up to whatever is out there. When we do this, just about anything can and does come through in our visions. More often than not, what comes through is something less than pure Goddess or God consciousness. Attuning the bowl or any psychic tool to the energies of the Goddess and God helps to assure that spiritual work is indeed divine.

Items Needed:

- Two candles—one black, one white.
- Dark Moon oil.[11]
- At least ½ oz. of dried rose petals.
- An incense burner and an incense charcoal already lit.
- A small amount of sea salt and a small container of clear water.

Using the rose petals, mark out a circle two feet in diameter on the floor. Place your newly decorated black bowl in the center and place the two candles on opposing edges of the circle, one in the east, one in the west. Since the east is traditionally the place of knowledge, place the white candle at that compass point. The west is typically the place of intuition, so there we will place the black candle, our candle of mystery.

Consecrate the water by holding your hands over or in the filled water container, saying:

Be thou holy by the names of Hecate and Cernunnos.

Continue by consecrating the salt in the same manner. Hold your hands over the salt and say:

Be thou holy by the names of Hecate and Cernunnos.

Anoint the black bowl with both the salt and the water, saying each time:

Thou art consecrated by the powers of _____ .
                                     (water or earth)

Sprinkle a few rose petals on the burning charcoal, then pick up the bowl and turn it upside down. Hold it over the smoldering rose petals and allow the inside of the bowl to fill with smoke. Turn it right side up, allowing the smoke to dissipate, while saying:

Thou art consecrated by the powers of air.

Next, light the white and black candles, and hold the bowl over each one for a few moments, saying:

Thou art consecrated by the powers of fire.

Finally, take a dab of the Dark Moon oil on the tip of a finger and touch it to the center of the bowl. Begin to create a counterclockwise spiral that ends at the top lip of the bowl. While you do this, chant the following:

Vessel of holy visions, be thou sacred!
Vessel of holy visions, be thou divine!
Vessel of holy visions, mystery revealed!
Vessel of holy visions, be thou mine!

Next you'll want to create specially charged waters for the vision work of the black bowl.

DISTILLING THE SACRED WATERS

Moon Phase: 3rd quarter.

Purpose: creating sacred waters for the black bowl.

Items Needed:

- The following dried herbs: rose petals, sea salt, jasmine, and hyssop. (If you can find dried jimson weed—*Datura stramonium*—include some of this too. Be very careful not to consume any of this highly poisonous herb.)
- A large, clear bottle or jar.

Take out your large, clear bottle on a day of the third quarter of the waning moon. In a separate mixing bowl, stir together the herbs. Mix this together with the water—one part herb mixture to four parts of the water. Stir in three teaspoons of sea salt.

Pour the mixture into your clear glass jar or clear, covered bowl, somewhere in a sunny spot where it will be undisturbed, allowing the power of the sun and moon to distill the waters and blend with the herbs. Allow them to blend and steep until the last night of the fourth quarter of the waning moon—the time of the dark moon. This process will last anywhere from nine to sixteen days, so you'll want to check on the sacred water periodically, just to see if the water levels are still high. If the water looks too low, go ahead and add another one-half to ¾ cup of fresh water.

The waters have been charged by the sun and moon, so there is no need to lend personal energy to the mixture. When the final day has arrived, strain off the herb particles until all that remains is a clear, brownish liquid that looks somewhat like tea. Save this water in a bottle or jar for your divination.

BLACK BOWL DIVINATIONS

On a dark moon night, go outside with the black bowl and your container of sacred divination water. Fill the bowl with the water and peer into the surface, allowing your conscious mind to drift off. What do you see?

DARK MOON MAGIC: CURSES AND BINDINGS

Witches and shamans should be aware that the dark moon is a time for cursing as well as healing. It is important to know this because even though Witches are never cursers, there are hurt and misguided people who actively engage in harming others with psychic energy. I have never met anyone who admits to cursing, but I have heard occasional stories of those who have been assaulted magically. Evidence of magical attack may include increased, unexplainable restlessness, fatigue, depression, increased emotional negativity, withdrawal from those who may be able to help, and a feeling of heaviness[12] surrounding you.

Wise Folk who are aware of this protect themselves from potential harm by using what is called a binding. Magical bindings are spells that deflect negative energies and return them to their point of origin. They halt the attacker from harming anyone. But why shouldn't you attack back? Why not get retribution?

The Wiccan Rede, the law that governs the Craft, proclaims, "An' it harm none, do as ye wilt." Witches do not curse because they are healers and live in harmony with nature. Cursers live against nature. They do not trust the natural order of the Universe and take the laws of karma into their own hands. This is a very dangerous affair, for the principle of "threefold return" governs magical operations. This principle says that whatever you do magically to someone else will come back to you three times over.

Bindings are in line with the workings of the Craft, with nature, and with the Gods, because they are transformative magic. They change a destructive situation into a neutral one. Bindings return life to a state of natural balance.

I have begun this section on Dark Moon Magic with binding spells that are quick and effective. I have only had to use bindings twice in my magical career, but both times were successful and transformative.

The Three Times Three Spell

Moon Phase: 3rd quarter.

Purpose: to rid the physical, emotional, or spiritual planes of negative energy sent by another (whether intentionally or not). Also to stop the negative activity of others who may be harming you or someone you love. Brings forth balance.

Items Needed:

- A black candle (or better yet, a black figure candle; use either male or female if you know the gender of the one sending negativity your way).
- A small spool of cotton twine.
- A small amount of lamp oil (or essential oil mixed with a base, like grapeseed oil).

- A cauldron or deep dish to contain the candle.
- Sand.
- A small, sharp knife, or Witch's athame.

Use your athame to inscribe the name of the person, or a word symbolizing the negative situation near the bottom of the candle. Place the candle between your palms and breathe onto the figure three times. With each breath, imagine you are exhaling the negativity you have received onto the candle.

Take the cotton twine and tie it around the base of the candle, so that at least two feet of twine hangs from the knot. Begin tightly coiling the twine around the candle or figure in a counter-clockwise direction. While doing so visualize a giant, protective, mirrored egg surrounding you and repeatedly chant:

> Three times three, as ye have sown
> Is thine to reap, thy harvest grown.
> For best, for worst, for praise or chide,
> The Gods alone your fate decide!

Continue wrapping the candle with the twine until you have spiraled to the top, covering every bit of the candle. Loop the string, tying it in a knot to one of the coils at the top near the wick. Next take the lamp oil or essential oil blend and liberally smear the twine and candle with it. Be sure to cover every inch of the entwined candle. Next, pour sand into the cauldron or container, wedge the candle into the sand so that it stands erect, and light it on fire. Watch as the candle melts away, knowing that the magical attack has been deflected.

The Wax Poppet

A poppet is a human representation, a doll-like figure used to symbolize a person at whom magic is aimed. Poppets are typically used in cursing and bindings, but they are also effective in healing and love spells. Spells that incorporate poppets have a certain reputation about them because the use of human-like imagery in magic is so evocative. The use of such a tool signifies serious magical business.

In this spell, you will make an image of someone who means you harm, so it is most effective if you have seen the magical aggressor at least once.

Moon Phase: 3rd or 4th.

Purpose: to bind a magical attacker.

Items Needed:

- A chunk of beeswax (the more you have of this, the larger the doll).
- A pentagram at least five inches in diameter (can be drawn on paper).

- Five red votive candles.
- The following herbs ground together into a powder: aconite, mandrake, and fern (if possible, hellebore and hemlock—be careful, though since they are extremely poisonous).
- A jar with a lid large enough to accommodate your figure.
- A length of red thread, cord, or ribbon long enough to wrap around the figure several times.

Begin by warming up the beeswax. You can do this in a microwave oven or on a conventional stove. In a microwave, it is best to warm the wax using only 50% wattage. The purpose is simply to make the wax pliable, not melted.

The same rule applies to warming the wax over a conventional stove. I have found it easier to select a very small pan that I only use for warming wax, because once the wax gets soft, it can get all over the pan and it is very difficult to clean out. Warm the wax over low heat for a few minutes. Test it every now and then for plasticity.

Once it is supple enough, take it out of the microwave or pan and begin to shape the wax into a human figure. At this point, there are other traditional items you can incorporate into the figure to establish a strong psychic link between the poppet and the person it represents. Traditional spells of this nature call for such items as hair, nail clippings, a piece of fabric from the person's clothing, pieces of the person's photograph, or any other item with which the magical attacker has had contact. Adding these items is not a necessity, but if it rouses your unconscious mind toward power, you might try it.

As you work on shaping the figure, imagine that it is actually becoming the person whom it represents. Continue working on it until you have as much or as little detail as your unconscious needs. Allow your intuition to tell you when to stop.

Once you are done, hold the figure in your hands, and present it to each of the four quarters. Start by facing the west, saying at each direction:

> Waves and flames, winds and soil,
> Spiral now within;
> Cerridwen's dark cauldron boil,
> Let the spell begin!

Now place the figure at the center of your pentagram and put the five red votive candles at each point of the star. Light each of the five candles in turn. Light the first one, then sprinkle a pinch of the powdered herb mixture on the figure's feet, saying:

Feet bound!

After you light the second one, sprinkle a pinch more on the poppet's legs, saying:

Knees bound!

Light the third one, and sprinkle more of the herbs onto the pelvis of the figure, saying:

(Womb/Phallus) bound!

Continue by lighting the forth one, then sprinkling herbs onto the poppet's chest, saying:

Breast bound!

Light the last candle and then sprinkle the last pinch of herbs onto the poppet's head, saying:

Harm bound!

Finally, wrap the figure several times over with your twine, thread, or ribbon. As you do this chant:

Twine will seal the magic's might,
Harm will fade with morning's light.
May all things be as I appoint,
And bane return to the starting point!

The spell is now completed. To keep the magic strong, place the figure in a jar or box and store it safely away. You will never have trouble from that person again.

The Healing Vortex

When you are in need of healing, the influence of the dark moon can be helpful. Sometimes while sick, it is difficult to conjure up positive, healing images for ourselves. Instead, here is a method that conjures up negative imagery and then neutralizes it. Remember, the power of the waning moon is that of drawing out and of ending. Our focus is on ending the sickness.

Moon Phase: 4th quarter.

Purpose: to halt an illness.

Items Needed:

- ◐ Dried lavender, sage, and hyssop (a tablespoon each).
- ◐ A bathtub.
- ◐ Patchouli or rose essential oil.
- ◐ A tablespoon each of sea salt and baking soda.

Fill a bathtub with hot water. Be certain that the water is not so hot that you will not be able to ease your entire body into the tub. But the temperature should be hot enough to initially make you feel mildly uncomfortable—in other words, it should be a few degrees above your normal bath temperature.

After the bath is drawn, before you climb in, hold your hands just above the water and recite the following incantation three times:

> **This is Cerridwen's cauldron;**
> **The mists of change arise!**

Take the lavender and hold it in your hands above the water for a moment, saying:

> **Lavender for love!**

Sprinkle the lavender into the water. Take the sage and in the same manner, say:

> **Sage for strength!**

After sprinkling the sage into the water, take the hyssop in the same manner, saying:

> **Hyssop for healing!**

Sprinkle the hyssop into the water and add a few drops of the essential oils.

This next step is important. With your hand, athame, wand, or even a large wooden spoon, stir the waters widdershins to create a vortex of downward, drawing energy. As you stir the waters, chant:

> **Flowers and water keep sickness at bay;**
> **The downward spiral takes it away!**

Use the chanting and your imagination to help create the downward drawing energy. There is no set rule as to when to stop stirring and chanting; it is best to use your intuition, as it is different for each person. Generally it lasts no longer than several minutes.

Next, carefully ease yourself into the waters.[13] Imagine while you are soaking that all of the negativity is oozing out of your pores. It seeps out of your skin and out of your lungs with each breath. It mingles with the water and herbs. Imagine this for as long as you can. If you can keep this up for thirty minutes or so, you will effect the healing.

The Spell of the Ancestral Spirits

Our ancestors live in our veins. Everything from the shape of our bodies to the world we live in was first touched by many before us. They live in our hearts, so whenever we have need of their assistance, we may call upon their presence to guide us or even to intercede on our behalf.

Moon Phase: 3rd or 4th quarter.

Purpose: to elicit the aid of ancestral spirits to achieve any magical intent.

Items Needed:

- A mirror.
- Two white or two brown[14] candles.
- A handful of earth.
- A bell.

In order to effectively work this spell, select a secret symbol or rune that will symbolize your magical intent. For instance, if you were to summon ancestral aid for assistance in a relationship, you might select the glyph of Venus, the planet in astrology that rules relationships and love.

Below are listed some astrological glyphs and their symbolic spheres of influence. Feel free to use any type of symbol, sigil, or rune that is meaningful to you.

- ☉ (Sun)—Generosity, wealth, longevity, health, prosperity, happiness.

- ☽ (Moon)—Home, hearth, family, emotions, tides, ebbs and flows, business, psychic prowess, women's mysteries.

♂ (Mars)—Aggression, passion, lust, anger, war, strength, endurance, action, men's mysteries.

♀ (Venus)—Love, artistry, balance, partnerships, possessions, money, social life, beauty, adornment.

☿ (Mercury)—Intellect, communication, travel, transportation, the rational mind, knowledge, learning.

♃ (Jupiter)—Philosophy, religious matters, speculation, higher learning, expansion, good fortune.

♄ (Saturn)—Karma, law, slow change, tenacity, perseverance, restriction, hard work.

On a night of the waning moon, just before midnight, the hour of the Crone and Sage, take out your mirror and place it flat on a table's surface in front of you. You may wish to do this in the construct of your magic circle. In that case, place the mirror flat on your altar. Be sure you have a chair so that you can sit at the table or altar for a while.

Next, place the two candles on opposing sides of the mirror. They don't have to be touching the mirror—leave enough room on either side so that you can gaze down into the mirror without getting burned.

Ring your bell thirteen times. The number thirteen in this enchantment signifies that you are moving beyond the midnight hour, into a zone that is beyond the limits of time.

Hold the handful of dirt in your left hand, face the west, raise your arms out, invoking:

> **Blood red roots. Time is no thing beyond your bounds. And crimson is the open earth, the womb grave, the body grove, where blood red roots rest. Awaken and come to me grandmothers and children, for I ask a boon of thee tonight.**

Then spread the handful of dirt onto the surface of the Mirror. Draw a magical sigil that pertains to your reason for inquiry in the dirt. Hold your hands over the dirt-covered glass and chant:

> **Come oh come, my beloved be here.**
> **Come as the midnight hour draws near.**

Imagine the many loving ancestral spirits that enter your sacred space from the west and surround you with their aid.

To see their faces, brush the dirt away from the Mirror, starting at the edges and look down into the Mirror. Sometimes, on your own face, you will see the image of a long-dead relative.

To End a Relationship

Every relationship, whether you perceive it as positive or negative, is the product of karma. You enter into relationships with others because they present you with the issues your spirit requires to grow toward unity with the divine. Every person with whom you have contact reflects back to you aspects of yourself—positive, negative, or both. When you have challenging encounters, it is good to remember that you were drawn into this relationship for learning, for drawing you closer to resolution of your shadows.

There are relationships that are unhealthy and that no longer serve a higher good. They are simply harmful physically, emotionally, or spiritually. If you find yourself in a destructive relationship, it is for your own higher good and growth to cut the karmic relationship ties and move on with your life without the other person.

Although cutting ties to another can hurt, this working is a celebration of renewal, of reawakening to spiritual health and well-being.

Moon Phase: 3rd quarter (do this rite shortly after the full moon).

Purpose: to cut karmic ties in a destructive relationship.

Items Needed:

◗ A fresh, red rose.

- A cauldron or container that can contain a small fire *safely*. Whatever vessel you use, it *must* be able to withstand extreme heat without breaking or cracking. This is crucial. If you do not have access to this type of burning vessel, do not attempt this magical working.
- A handful of dried pennyroyal.
- A few dried feverfew flowers.
- A handful of dried sage.
- A figure candle (your choice of color).
- Denatured alcohol. (Any well-stocked home improvement store will carry this.)
- A Witch's athame or other sharp knife.
- Dark Moon oil.

It is important that you do this working out of doors because the fumes of the denatured alcohol should not be breathed in directly. Also, this ritual requires the use of fire, so proceed with caution. Be sure there is no underbrush nearby that can accidentally catch fire. Before working, place a heat-tempered ceramic tile or dish underneath your burning vessel for fire safety.

Choose a figure candle that best suits your situation. If a figure candle cannot be acquired, use a taper of an appropriate color. With your athame or sharp knife, inscribe the sigils of Venus and Saturn both at the top and bottom of the candle.

Venus: ♀   Saturn: ♄

Next, dress the candle by smearing it completely with Dark Moon oil. Fill the cauldron or burning vessel with ⅛ cup of denatured alcohol. Place the wax figure into the burning vessel with the denatured alcohol. Light a single match, stand clear of the cauldron or vessel, and *carefully* toss the lit match into the denatured alcohol. This will immediately ignite, so proceed with caution. While the candle melts in the flames chant:

> Tip the lover's cup and flow
> The waters of our blending.
> Seed returns to seed and so
> Our time has come for ending.

While this fire burns, grind the three dried herbs together into a powder in the mortar. Using the powdered herb mix, create a two-foot circle on the ground around the burning vessel with the candle in the middle of it.

Take out your red rose. Hold it over the cauldron and cut off the bloom. The spell is done. Take whatever positive actions are required to terminate the relationship meaningfully.

Co End Poverty

In this working, you will clear away the psychic dead wood of the past, such as poverty and ill luck, to foster a new cycle of growth and prosperity. It clears away the psychic dross that keeps you from taking the actions needed to create a prosperous life. Remember, abundance flows from the Goddess and God. They are abundance. Connecting with the Gods in their aspect of abundance is connecting with that same part of yourself. When you yield to nature, to the Gods, nature will yield its bounty to you.

Moon Phase: 4th quarter—last night of the dark moon.

Purpose: to end a cycle of lack.

Items Needed:

- The following dried herbs and resins: powdered sandalwood, pine needles, rosemary, and copal.
- Fresh rose petals.
- Optional: saltpetre.
- White parchment paper.
- A box of crayons, colored pencils, or markers.
- An incense burner, chafing dish, or cauldron.
- A self-igniting charcoal (Three Kings brand).
- The usual tools for constructing a magic circle.[15]

On the last night of the dark moon gather your herbs, combine them in a mortar, and grind them together. Make as much as you like, but you will only use about one tablespoon of the dried mixture total. After mixing, set it aside for a moment.

Next create a circle on the floor using the fresh rose petals. Bring all of your ingredients and tools into the rose petal circle and cast a dark moon circle, using the petals as the boundary of the sacred space.

Once the circle is cast, set aside all of your tools and sit in the circle's center. Do the following meditation before continuing with the magical work.

Ending Poverty Meditation

There is a place deep inside of you where poverty lives. Close your eyes and take a few slow, relaxing breaths. Imagine that you are traveling inside your body to that place where poverty lives. Take note of where that place is inside of you. Also take note of what this entity—poverty—looks like. What is its shape and color? What does it say to you? When you have taken note of all of this, return to waking consciousness and continue with the magical working.

Using the crayons, markers, or colored pencils, draw the image of poverty you saw on the white parchment paper. Underneath that image, make a list of the effects of lack on your life. How does poverty manifest in your life? The next step is a little more difficult, but on that same page make a list of the things you do to help keep poverty alive. What is your part in perpetuating poverty?

When you are done, sprinkle the herb mixture into the center of the parchment paper. If you choose to use saltpetre, sprinkle in a one-half teaspoon now. Twist the whole bundle shut, so that the parchment makes a little pouch containing the herb mix. Light the charcoal and set the paper-pouch on to the charcoal. Soon this will smoulder. As it does, imagine that the spirit of poverty is leaving your body. Imagine that you cut off all life support to poverty, imagine how you will not cooperate with it any longer.

When the herbs are completely burned, the spell is done. If any paper remains, light that on fire. Be certain that nothing but ashes remain.

Banish your circle and bury the ashes in a spot that you are not likely to tread upon. The magic is complete.

Notes

1. Scrying means to divine, to see the future.

2. Jacob and Wilhelm Grimm, *Fairy Tales*, New York: Alfred A. Knopf, (1992) from Edgar Taylor's translation of Grimms' *Kinder-und Haus-märchen*, (1823), p. 188.

3. This frame should have a stand or an easel-style back-prop that can keep it standing while you do your magical work. Many people choose frames that have Art Nouveau or gothic styling. Remember, the frame is part of the speculum, and you'll be looking at it whenever you use the mirror. It is best to choose something powerfully evocative, or aesthetically pleasing at the very least.

4. See Appendix B for incense recipe.

5. See Appendix B for oil recipe.

6. See Appendix A for instructions.

7. The Horned Lord is in reference to the ancient European deity Cernunnos, as I mentioned earlier in the book. He is also known as "Lord of the Hunt." In the aspect of the Dread Lord, the God is keeper of the underworld, guardian of death and rebirth.

8. The traditional herbs used in banishing the effects of a past life are baneful in nature and include a combination of hemlock, hellebore, deadly nightshade, and Solomon's Seal. These herbs are dangerous to use, and are listed here for historical interest only. Two friends have told me stories related to handling these herbs that should be taken under advisement. The first said that she placed a sprig of hemlock so that it had contact with her skin for twenty minutes or so. After that time, she noticed that a terrible rash had developed in the area that had contact. The second friend told me that he tried to burn a piece of hemlock and the smoke that emanated from the burning caused blisters to appear on the exposed parts of his skin. Since this spell includes the burning of herbs, I would not recommend burning any of these on the baneful list.

9. Saturn is the planet that governs karma.

10. Depending on which gender personifies your wisdom, use the corresponding terms, Crone or Sage, as before.

11. See Appendix B for recipe.

12. For those people who see rather than feel energy, it looks like a black cloud has enshrouded you.

13. It is important to note that you should not stay in the waters if the heat is unbearable. Add some cool water to the bath until it is tolerable.

14. Brown is the color that represents Earth. Symbolically, with the brown candle, we are asking our ancestors to manifest themselves.

15. See Appendix A for circle construction.

Appendices

Appendix A

WIDDERSHINS OR DARK MOON CIRCLE CASTING AND BANISHING

The following ritual format is meant to be a guideline only. It can be used as it stands; however, the purpose of ritual is to address the issues, moods, and sensations of the moment. Therefore, rituals change and shift from time to time so that they can be living, breathing extensions of yourself.

Once you have practiced this ritual a few times, you will be able to clearly see where alterations, additions, or subtractions can be made. Be creative and spontaneous with your alterations. Remember, rituals come from the spirit, which is fluid and changeable, so diversity and ease should be your main guidelines in constructing your rituals.

Before you start a ritual, you might need a transition period. This is the process of grounding or centering your consciousness.

GROUNDING AND CENTERING

Grounding and centering simply means finding the center of your being and anchoring everything else within to that center. The center is the internal balance point between the worlds of matter and spirit. Grounding and centering takes place before rituals to help you make the transition from mundane to spiritual consciousness.

Imagine that you are surrounded by complete blackness. The void swirls around you and draws you deep into your core, which is the dwelling place of the Gods. Once you arrive at your center, ask the Goddess and God for her or his protection in your dark moon circle. As you do so, imagine a deep purple field of light surrounding you. When you are ready, open your eyes and begin the next step, which is quartering the circle.

QUARTERING THE CIRCLE

Quartering the circle is marking out the physical space you will be using in your sacred rite by identifying the four compass directions. Claiming the space that will be consecrated is a herald to otherworld beings (the elementals we met in previous exercises, as well as deity) announcing your magical intentions. Quartering the circle symbolically prepares your consciousness for work with the dark moon powers: to accept, to surrender, to wonder, and to resonate.

Place four candles around the perimiter of your sacred space: one in the west, south, east, and north. Also, it is helpful to have candles with colors that correspond to the elements and directions. West is blue, south is red, east is yellow, north is green. Place these appropriately in the actual compass direction. The size of the sacred circle is unimportant[1] (so long as you have room to manuver without worrying about stepping outside of it). As you place each candle out, stand on the perimeter of your circle, just on the edge facing out.

Start the quartering process in the west, and as you place the blue candle down hold your arms outstretched, palms facing out, saying:

> May my sacred space be born from the waters of the west.
> Undines, mermaids, and all watery beings bring forth
> The power to accept.   *(dare)*   ←*(deosil)*

Light the candle and then move to the south of your circle. Set down the red candle, and as before, hold your arms up and say:

> May my sacred space be warmed by the fires of the south.
> Salamanders and all firey beings, bring forth
> The power to surrender.   (will)

Light that candle and then move to the east. After setting down the yellow candle, hold your arms up, saying:

> May my sacred space be animated by the breath of life,
> Gales from the east,
> Fairies, sylphs, and all airy beings, bring forth
> The power to wonder.   (know)

Light that candle and then go to the northern quarter. Set down the north's candle, then hold your arms up, saying:

> May my sacred space be created by the womb of the earth.
> O gnomes and all earthy beings, bring forth
> The power to resonate.   (to be silent)

Light that candle and then return to the west once again to connect the space together. While facing the west, hold your arms out one last time to close the space.

The use of gesture may feel awkward or overly theatrical at first, but gestures are yet another way of acting in a sacred manner in order to help us transition from one state of consciousness to another. They help summon the priestess and priest in each of us.

Once the space has been marked out, move to the next step, which is blessing each physical element to be used.

BLESSING OF ELEMENTS

Traditionally, contemporary Wiccans say their blessings, spells, and other enchantments in rhyme. Rhyme is easy to remember, which may explain its widespread use, but it also creates an air of the extraordinary. We don't normally speak in couplets. Doing so in a sacred setting helps facilitate consciousness changes.

If speaking in rhyme feels stilted, then make up your own words, or better yet, allow the silence to bless each element. Feel free to change the words at any time.

First, hold your hands over a bowl filled with water and say:

water

> Reveal to me, thou holy dew,
> The mysteries yet known to few.
> By secret pools in ink-black night,
> I summon now thy sacred might.

Next, use your finger to draw a spiral in the salt. While doing so, say:

salt

> Inspire within, thou blessed soil,
> The sacred spiral to uncoil.
> By mystic mounds in ink-black night,
> I summon now thy sacred might.

Next, light the red candle on your altar. This is the representation of the element of fire. Hold your hands near the flickering flame, saying:

fire

> Live within me blessed flames,
> I ask this in the holy names.
> By secret fires in ink-black night,
> I summon now thy sacred might.

Finally, place some incense[2], the representation of air, onto the lit charcoal, saying:

air

> Enchant for me, thou airy one,
> Thy sacred task has thus begun.
> By secret winds in ink-black night,
> I summon now thy sacred might.

After you have blessed each element, you will want to anoint yourself, which will help you align with them internally. Touch a dab of the salt and water to your brow, which is the third eye area, a center of great psychic sensitivity. Next, take the candle and hold it near the heart chakra, which, of course, is located in the center of your chest. Hold the smoldering incense close to the throat chakra and allow the smoke to waft over you. With each of these elemental blessings, you could add a verbal charge, such as:

> I am consecrated with the element of (air, fire, water, or earth).

widdershins
Casting the Circle

The next step in the process of creating a dark moon circle is called casting the circle. This process is quite possibly the oldest of ritual activities, going back to the beginnings of mythological thinking, which some scholars suggest began with the australopithecine, a primitive form of human evolutionary development[3] that emerged roughly four million years ago. When we cast the circle, we move between the worlds of the mundane and magical—we go beyond time and place.

Start by standing in the west, facing the perimeter of your circle. Take a few deep, slow breaths. As you breathe, imagine that the purple aura lent to you by the Gods begins to fill your lungs. From your lungs, the aura fills your feet, your legs, your pelvis, chest, arms, hands, neck, and head. Feel the pressure of the magical aura building within you as you visualize and breathe. Once you are filled with this magical power, outstretch your arms, once again, to touch the fringe of your sacred space. Begin walking the edge of the circle widdershins: west to south to east to north. Imagine the aura emanating from your hands to build a psychic perimeter. As you do this, say:

> **I summon the circle, the circle I summon**
> **Power and peace and protection will come in**
> **And bind to the womb of our spiritual birth**
> **Through water and fire and air and earth.**

The last ritual gesture you will perform is that of summoning the powers of the elements. In this case, you will be summoning the widdershins powers. To do this successfully, you will be drawing a series of invoking pentagrams in the air using your athame or your hand. When you close the circle, you will draw the pentagrams again, but they will be reversed, so that their effect is banishing. The appropriate invoking and banishing pentagrams are diagramed at the end of this section.

Start by facing the west. Draw an invoking pentagram of water, saying:

> **Deep, rolling, moving, shifting,**
> **Sparkleless in the moon's void.**
> **Finned ones, bring forth the power to accept.**

Now move to the south. Draw an invoking pentagram of fire, saying:

Dark flame's center beyond centers,
All that is and isn't is kissed by you.
Burning ones, bring forth the power to surrender.

Move to the east. Draw an invoking pentagram of air and say:

Howling spirits, haunting gales,
All that was once known—blow away.
Winged ones, bring forth the power to wonder.

Finally, go to the north. Draw an invoking pentagram of earth and say:

Solid, cold, silent wise ones,
That which voids begin to fill.
Earthy ones, bring forth the power to resonate.

Your circle is now complete. At this time, it is appropriate to do magical workings or sacred inner-journeys. Once you have completed this magical work, celebrate with the traditional Wiccan cakes and wine. Any type of post-ritual feasting is appropriate because it helps you to ground and center once again. Bless the food you consume in the names of the Gods or the elements.

Banishing the Circle

Once your magical or meditation work is completed, it is time to close the circle. The procedure for this is simply to reverse the process of circle construction. In other words, everything that was invited to the circle is dismissed, everything summoned is released.

Begin by banishing all elemental powers summoned. Stand in each quarter: west, south, east, and north in turn. Draw a banishing pentagram at each and say:

Farewell to thee, guardians of the west (south, east, north).
Leave from us here. Return to thy sphere!

After you draw the banishing pentagrams, snuff out each quarter candle.

Finally, you will banish the formal circle. To begin, stand once again in the west, facing out. Hold your arms out again, close your eyes and imagine that you draw the energies of the circle within you. Walk the perimeter of the circle, but this time traverse the sacred space in a deosil way: west, north, east, south, and back once again to the west. As you banish the circle, say:

> Earth will crumble my circle,
> Winds will tear at the clay,
> Fire will burn what's left in the urn,
> And water will wash it away.

This completes the banishing of your dark moon circle.

DEOSIL CIRCLE CASTING AND BANISHING

This is meant to be a guide in creating sacred space during the waxing moon. Feel free to experiment and change the words of power anywhere in the text, for it is best to find words of power that resonate with your own magical sensibilities.

Items Needed:

- Salt.
- Water.
- An athame.
- A red candle.
- Incense.
- Four candles representing the four quarters.

CIRCLE CASTING

Place your four quarter candles around the working space, one at each of the compass directions. If you are using colored candles, place the yellow one in the east, the red in the south, the blue in the west, and the green in the north. (Otherwise use all white, since white contains all colors.)

Next place your altar[4] at the center of your circle. On it position the salt, or earth, on the north side of the altar; put the incense in the east, the red fire candle in the south, and the bowl of water in the west.

Light each of the quarter candles in turn, starting in the east and moving deosil.

Return to the altar and hold your athame over the bowl of water, saying:

> I consecrate thee, o creature of water
> In the names of the Great Mother and the Horned One.

Hold your athame over the salt, saying:

> I consecrate thee, o creature of earth
> In the names of the Great Mother and the Horned One.

Using your athame, scoop three small heaps of salt into the water and stir. Take the saltwater to the edge of the circle and sprinkle it all along the perimeter.

Return to the altar. Hold your athame over the fire candle, saying:

> I consecrate thee, o creature of fire
> In the names of the Great Mother and the Horned One.

Hold the athame over the lit incense, saying:

> I consecrate thee, o creature of air
> In the names of the Great Mother and the Horned One.

Take the candle to the edge of the circle and take it around the perimeter. Do the same with the incense.

Next, touch yourself with the water and salt mixture at the third eye, saying:

> Blessed am I with the virtues of water and earth.

Hold the candle and the incense near the third eye, saying:

> Blessed am I with the virtues of fire and air.

Next you shall cast the formal circle, which will require all of your concentration. Stand in the east and point your athame outward to the edge of the circle. Walk clockwise, pointing the blade outward, and make one complete circle (returning to the east), saying:

> I summon the circle, the circle I summon
> Power and peace and protection will come in
> And bind to the womb of our spiritual birth
> Through air and fire and water and earth.

Next you will invoke the powers of the elements at each of the four compass directions. To do this succcessfully, you will be drawing a series of invoking pentagrams in the air using your athame or your hand. When you close the circle, you will draw the pentagrams again, but they will be reversed, so that their effect is banishing. Start in the eastern quarter by drawing an invoking pentagram in the air (with your athame or your hand) and say:

> O sylphs of the wind, I ask thee to blow
> And bring on thy wings the power to know!

In the southern quarter, draw an invoking pentagram and say:

> Salamanders of fire, I call thee
> Until you bring on thy flames the power to will!

In the west, draw an invoking pentagram, saying:

> O undines of water, come as I declare
> And bring on thy waves the power to dare!

In the north, draw your final invoking pentagram and say:

> O gnomes of the earth, I ask thee aright,
> Bring from thy mountains the silence of night!

Return to your altar and face east. Now you will invoke the God and Goddess. Raise your arms skyward and say:

> Hear me ancient ones! Lady of the Moon, Lord of the Sun,
> Descend, I pray, into this my circle.
> Be with me now to lend thy blessings.

This completes the casting of the circle.

CIRCLE BANISHING

Draw a banishing pentagram in the east, saying:

> Farewell to thee, guardians of the east.
> Leave from us here! Return to thy sphere!

Draw a banishing pentagram in the south, saying:

> Farewell to thee, guardians of the south.
> Leave from us here! Return to thy sphere!

Draw a banishing pentagram in the west, saying:

> Farewell to thee, guardians of the west.
> Leave from us here! Return to thy sphere!

Draw a banishing pentagram in the north, saying:

> Farewell to thee, guardians of the north.
> Leave from us here! Return to thy sphere!

Next you will banish the formal circle. Hold your athame out while standing in the east. This time, walk widdershins, making one complete circle (that is, returning to the east), saying:

> Earth will crumble my circle,
> Water will cause it to fall,
> Fire will burn what's left in the urn,
> And the winds will scatter it all.

This completes the deosil circle banishing.

Invoking and Banishing Pentagrams

Pentagram of Spirit

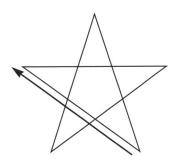

Invoking

Banishing

Pentagram of Fire

south

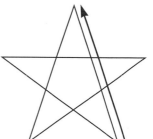

Invoking   Banishing

Pentagram of Earth

north

Invoking   Banishing

Pentagram of Air

east

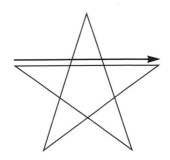

Invoking   Banishing

Pentagram of Water

west

Invoking   Banishing

Notes

1. Traditionally, however, the circle is measured out to be nine feet in diameter. If you choose to do this for traditional purposes, that is fine, but the measurement of the circle is not crucial to achieve spiritual development.

2. Use the recipe for Dark Moon incense given in Appendix B, or any other that seems to fit the mood of your ritual.

3. From a recorded lecture by the late Joseph Campbell: "Orgins of Man and Myth," in *The World of Joseph Campbell, Transformations of Myth through Time*, Mythology Ltd., 1989.

4. The altar can be any small table or box large enough to contain the necessary tools.

Appendix B

Incense and Oil Blends

These incense and oil blends are suggestions only. It is best to use whatever scents are evocative for you. If these blends don't seem to trigger you psychically, try other recipes. For additional recipes, see *The Complete Book of Incense, Oils and Brews* by Scott Cunningham.

Wisdom Incense

Dried herbs needed:

- ◑ ⅓ cup cinnamon (cassia) powder.

- ◑ ⅓ cup frankincense resin.

- ◑ ⅓ cup sandalwood powder.

- ◑ ⅛ cup lavender.

Blend these together in a mortar, then add in the following essential oils, stirring well:

- ◑ 2 drops cinnamon oil.

- ◑ 5 drops myrrh oil.

Wisdom Oil

Into ¼ cup of grapeseed oil, blend the following essential oils:

- ◑ 2 drops cinnamon oil.

- ◑ 4 drops myrrh oil.

- ◑ 3 drops lavender oil.

DARK MOON INCENSE

Blend the following dried herbs together:

- ¼ cup sandalwood powder.

- ⅛ cup patchouli.

- ½ cup myrrh.

To this add the following essential oils and stir together:

- 10 drops jasmine oil.

- 4 drops chamomile (or lemon) oil.

DARK MOON OIL

Into ¼ cup of grapeseed oil, blend the following essential oils:

- 7 drops jasmine.

- 2 drops chamomile (or lemon).

- 3 drops patchouli.

- 1 drop sandalwood.

Blessing Oil

Into safflower or grapeseed oil, blend the following herbs—one cup of oil to ½ cup of the following herb blend:

- ◑ 1 part juniper.
- ◑ 1 part basil.
- ◑ 1 part jasmine blossoms.

Set the mixture on a sunny windowsill for about two weeks. Strain out the herbs. To this oil blend in:

- ◑ 9 drops jasmine oil.

White Moon Incense

- ◑ ¼ cup willow powder.
- ◑ ¼ cup bamboo powder.
- ◑ ¼ cup copal resin "tears."

Stir this together and add the following essential oils:

- ◑ 3 drops lemon grass oil.
- ◑ 3 drops frankincense oil.
- ◑ 3 drops wisteria oil.

BIBLIOGRAPHY

BIBLIOGRAPHY

Afanasev, Aleksandr (Norbert Guterman, trans.). *Russian Fairy Tales*. New York: Pantheon Books, 1973.

Ardinger, Barbara. *A Woman's Book of Rituals and Celebrations*. San Rafael: New World Library, 1992.

Armstrong, Karen. *A History of God*. New York: Ballantine Books, 1994.

Baker, Donald. *Functions of Folk and Fairy Tales*. Washington, D.C.: Association for Childhood Education International, 1981.

Bellingham, David. *An Introduction to Celtic Mythology*. New Jersey: Chartwell Books, 1990.

Benedict, Ruth F. "The Concept of the Guardian Spirit in North America." *Memoirs of the American Anthropological Association*. Menasha, WI, 1923, V. 29, p. 67.

Berndt, R. and C. "A Preliminary Report of Field Work in the Ooldea Region, Western South Australia." *Oceania*, XII (1942), p. 323.

Bettelheim, Bruno. *The Uses of Enchantment*. New York: Alfred A. Knopf, Inc., 1977.

Calvino, Italo (George Martin, trans.). *Italian Folktales*. New York: Harcourt Brace Jovanovich, Inc., 1980.

Campbell, Joseph. *The Hero With A Thousand Faces*. New York: Princeton University Press, 1973.

———. *The Inner Reaches of Outer Space*. New York: Harper & Row, 1986.

———. *Transformations of Myth through Time*. New York: Harper & Row, 1990

Chodron, Pima. *Start Where You Are.* Boston: Shambhalah, 1994.

His Holiness the Dali Lama, *A Policy of Kindness: An Anthology of Writings by and about the Dali Lama.* New York: Snow Lion, 1990.

Davies, Paul. *The Mind of God.* New York: Touchstone, 1992.

Dieckman, Hans. *Twice Told Tales: The Psychological Aspects of Fairy Tales.* Wilmette: Chiron Publications, 1986.

Ellenberger, Henri F. *The Discovery of the Unconscious.* New York: Basic Books, 1970.

Fox, Matthew. *Original Blessing.* Santa Fe: Bear and Co., 1983.

Frazer, James G. *The Golden Bough.* New York: Avenel Books, 1924.

Gimbutas, Marija. *Gods and Goddesses of Old Europe.* Los Angeles: University of California Press, 1982.

———. *The Language of the Goddess,* San Francisco: Harper San Francisco, 1989.

Grimm, Jacob and Wilhelm. *Fairy Tales.* (based on translations by Edgar Taylor, 1823, and Marian Edwardes, 1901) New York: Alfred A. Knopf, Inc., 1992.

Grimm, Jakob, and Wilhelm Grimm. *Grimm's Other Tales.* South Brunswick, New Jersey: A.S. Barnes, 1966

Hannah, Thomas. *Somatics.* New York: Addison-Wesley Publishing Company, 1988.

Harner, Michael. *The Way of the Shaman.* New York: Bantam Books, 1986.

Hastings, Arthur C. Ph. D., James Fadiman, Ph.D., and James S. Gordon, M.D., *Health for the Whole Person.* Boulder, CO.: Westview Press, 1980.

Heusher, Julius E. *A Psychiatric Study of Fairy Tales.* Springfield: Thomas, 1963.

Highwater, Jamake. *The Primal Mind.* New York: Meridian, 1982.

Jacoby, Mario, Verena Kast and Ingrid Riedel, *Witches, Ogres and the Devil's Daughter.* Boston: Shambhala Publications, 1978.

Jacobs, Joseph. *English Folk and Fairy Tales.* (3rd edition, revised). New York: G.P. Putnam's Sons, (n.d.).

Jason, Heda, and Dimitri Segal, *Patterns in Oral Literature.* Chicago: Aldine, 1977.

Johnson, Sonia. *Going Out of Our Minds: The Metaphysics of Liberation.* Freedom: Crossing Press, 1987.

Jung, C.G. *Man and His Symbols.* New York: Doubleday, 1964.

Jung, C.G. R.F.C. Hull (trans.), Joseph Campbell (ed.), *The Portable Jung.* New York: Viking Press, 1971.

Khan, Masud R. "The Changing Use of Dreams in Psychoanalytic Practice," *International Journal of Psycho-Analysis.* 1976.

King, James Roy. *Old Tales and New Truths.* Albany: State University of New York Press, 1992.

Kready, Laura Fry. *A Study of Fairy Tales.* Boston: Houghton Mifflin, 1916.

Kurtines, William, and Jacob Gewirtz, *Moral Development Through Social Interaction.* New York: John Wiley & Sons, 1989.

Kurtz, Ron, and Hector Prestera, M.D. *The Body Reveals.* New York: Harper & Row, 1984.

Lowrey, Shirley Park. *Familiar Mysteries.* New York: Oxford University Press, 1982.

Lüthi, Max. *Once Upon A Time: On the Nature of Fairy Tales.* New York: F. Unger Publishing Co., 1970.

Malandro, Loretta, Larry Barker and Deborah Barker, *Nonverbal Communication.* New York: Random House, 1983.

Murray, Margaret. *The God of the Witches.* New York: Oxford University Press, 1970.

Muten, Burleigh. *Word Magic.* copyright 1993 Burleigh Muten.

Rico, Gabriele Lusser. *Writing the Natural Way.* New York: J.P. Tarcher, Inc., 1983.

Roderick, Timothy. *The Once Unknown Familiar.* St. Paul: Llewellyn Publications, 1994.

Rutherford, Ward. *Celtic Mythology.* New York: Sterling Publishing, 1990.

Sargent, Denny. *Global Ritualism.* St. Paul: Llewellyn Publications, 1994.

David Clement Scott, *A Cyclopaedic Dictionary of the Mang'anja Language Spoken in British Central Africa.* Edinburgh, 1892.

Simpson, D. P. *Cassell's Latin and English Dictionary.* New York: MacMillan Publishing, 1987.

Small, Jacqueline. *Awakening In Time.* New York: Bantam Books, 1991.

Sproul, Barbara. *Primal Myths.* San Francisco: Harper San Francisco, 1991.

Starhawk. *The Spiral Dance.* San Francisco: HarperCollins, 1989.

———. *Truth or Dare.* San Francisco: Harper & Row, 1987.

Steiger, Brad. *Kahuna Magic.* Gloucester, MA: Para Research, 1971.

Tolkien, J.R.R. *Tree and Leaf.* Boston: Houghton Mifflin, 1965.

Victor, Jeffrey S. *The Satanic Panic.* Chicago: Open Court Books, 1993.

Wellwood, John (ed.). *Awakening the Heart.* Boston: Shambhala Press, 1985.

White, Michael, David Epston, *Narrative Means to Therapeutic Ends.* New York: W.W. Norton & Co., 1990.

Zipes, Jack. *The Brothers Grimm.* London: Routledge, 1988.

————. (translator), *Beauties, Beasts and Enchantments.* New York: Meridian, 1991.

Sᴛᴀʏ ɪɴ Ꞇᴏᴜᴄʜ. . .

Llewellyn publishes hundreds of books on your favorite subjects

On the following pages you will find listed some books now available on related subjects. Your local bookstore stocks most of these and will stock new Llewellyn titles as they become available. We urge your patronage.

Order by Phone

Call toll-free within the U.S. and Canada, 1–800–THE MOON.
In Minnesota call (612) 291–1970.
We accept Visa, MasterCard, and American Express.

Order by Mail

Send the full price of your order (MN residents add 7% sales tax) in U.S. funds to:

> Llewellyn Worldwide
> P.O. Box 64383, Dept. K345–X
> St. Paul, MN 55164–0383, U.S.A.

Postage and Handling

- • $4.00 for orders $15.00 and under
- • $5.00 for orders over $15.00
- • No charge for orders over $100.00

We ship UPS in the continental United States. We cannot ship to P.O. boxes. Orders shipped to Alaska, Hawaii, Canada, Mexico, and Puerto Rico will be sent first-class mail.

International orders: Airmail—add freight equal to price of each book to the total price of order, plus $5.00 for each non-book item (audiotapes, etc.). Surface mail—Add $1.00 per item. Allow 4–6 weeks delivery on all orders. Postage and handling rates subject to change.

Group Discounts

We offer a 20% quantity discount to group leaders or agents. You must order a minimum of 5 copies of the same book to get our special quantity price.

FREE CATALOG

Get a free copy of our color catalog, *New Worlds of Mind and Spirit*. Subscribe for just $10.00 in the United States and Canada ($20.00 overseas, first-class mail). Many bookstores carry *New Worlds*—ask for it!

The Once Unknown Familiar
Shamanic Paths to Unleash Your Animal Powers

Timothy Roderick

Discover the magical animal of power residing within you! Animal "Familiars" are more than just the friendly animals kept by witches—the animal spirit is an extension of the unconscious mind, which reveals its power to those who seek its help. By using the detailed rituals, meditations, exercises and journaling space provided within this workbook, you will tap into the long-forgotten Northern European heritage of the "Familiar Self," and invoke the untamed, transformative power of these magical beasts.

This book focuses on traditional Northern European shamanic means of raising power—including drumming, dancing and construction of animal "fetiches"—and provides a grimoire of charms, incantations and spells anyone can work with a physical animal presence to enhance love, money, success, peace and more.

This is the first how-to book devoted exclusively to working with physical and spiritual Familiars as an aid to magic. Get in touch with your personal animal power, and connect with the magical forces of nature to effect positive change in your life and the lives of those around you.

0–87542–439–2, 240 pgs., 6 x 9, softcover $10.00

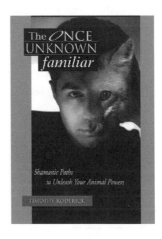

MOON MAGICK
MYTH & MAGIC, CRAFTS & RECIPES, RITUALS & SPELLS

D.J. Conway

No creature on this planet is unaffected by the power of the Moon. Its effects range from making us feel energetic or adventurous to tense and despondent. By putting excess Moon energy to work for you, you can learn to plan projects, work and travel at the optimum times.

Moon Magick explains how each of the 13 lunar months is directly connected with a different type of seasonal energy flow and provides modern rituals and spells for tapping this energy and celebrating the Moon phases. Each chapter describes new Pagan rituals—79 in all—related to that particular Moon, plus related Moon lore, ancient holidays, spells, meditations and suggestions for foods, drinks and decorations to accompany your Moon rituals. This book includes two thorough dictionaries of Moon deities and symbols.

By moving through the year according to the 13 lunar months, you can become more attuned to the seasons, the Earth and your inner self. *Moon Magic* will show you how to let your life flow with the power and rhythms of the Moon to benefit your physical, emotional and spiritual well-being.

ISBN: 1-56718-167-8, 7 x 10, 320 pp., illus., softbound $14.95

Between the Worlds
Witchcraft and the Tree of Life:
A Program of Spiritual Development

Stuart Myers

Embark upon the magickal path of the Witch with this thought-provoking look at a Goddess-oriented Qabalah. Through a blend of science, philosophy and brilliant ritual, *Between the Worlds* provides Witches and Qabalists alike with a complete system of magickal practice based upon the Old Religion. Drawing upon Gardnerian Wicca as a framework for exploring the Tree of Life, *Between the Worlds* includes a working Book of Shadows complete with new versions of the Lesser Banishing Ritual, Middle Pillar, and other Qabalistic practices revised to fit a Wiccan perspective.

This exciting and unique book opens the doors to a realm of incredible mystery and beauty. By reinterpreting the Qabalah in Wiccan terms, *Between the Worlds* offers Wiccans a chance to explore the higher planes of magick long thought to be the exclusive domain of ceremonial magicians. Using common elements of traditional Craft practice and an explanation of the Tree of Life in clear and concise language, this book reveals the way for Wiccans to explore the Qabalah of the Queen of Heaven.

ISBN: 1-56718-480-4, 7 x 10, 256 pp., illus., softcover   **$17.95**

CAULDRON OF TRANSFORMATION
A NEW VISION OF WICCA
FOR MODERN PAGAN PRACTICE

Lady Sabrina

Thousands of people, tired of the politics and dogma of the Christian Church but longing for deity and spirituality, have found the answer in Co-Creation Spirituality, a progressive formulation of doctrine and ritual that bridges the gap between Wiccan-Pagan ideology and the original intent of the Christian mysteries.

Cauldron of Transformation refreshingly approaches spirituality from an unbiased view and proclaims the truth and beauty of all positive religions. It explains the finer points of Paganism and teaches you how to blend and combine the wisdom of different traditions into a living spiritual system of your own. You will be introduced to the origins, customs and beliefs of five religious traditions: Celtic Druidism, Buddhism, Christianity, Santeria and Shamanism.

This book also provides new and dynamic tools to help extend and expand personal spiritual awareness. One such tool, the Vessel of Creation, provides a method of actually talking to your deity and receiving an answer in return.

ISBN: 1-56718-600-9, 6 x 9, 320 pp., illus., photos, softbound $16.95

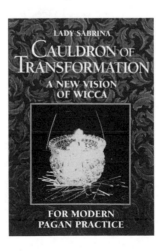

The Crone's Book of Words

Valerie Worth

The Crone's Book of Words contains rituals and spells to avert temptation, win another's love, recall one who is unfaithful, overcome insomnia, seek that which has been lost, atone for cutting down a tree, train a familiar, see the future, keep hair from falling, defeat tobacco, bring rain, and much more. Magic is alive, and Magic is afoot in the world today in the words spoken, read, sung, or only imagined. Here is Magic to enjoy and use: Magic to shape reality according to human will. Here is not the Magic of ceremony, of expensive robes and complex paraphernalia, nor of formulae calling for ingredients from the far ends of earth. This Magic is from the heart, this Magic sings in a woman's voice and is shaped with a woman's hands; it is the Magic incarnate in every woman for every woman knows of the Power within.

Valerie Worth—poet, wise woman, student of the occult—has created from her studies of Nature, Folklore and Magic these poems that are instructions, incantations and spells for nearly every purpose, from the personal to the universal. She bases her work on certain premises: that words themselves are a means to control exterior phenomena and interior changes; that magic today is the same craft that it has always been; and that all rituals spring from the same vision of life made meaningful.

0-87542-891-6, 160 pgs., 5-¼ x 8, illus., softcover   **$6.95**

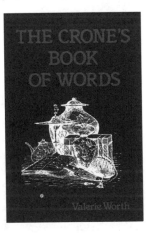

The Crone's Book of Wisdom

Valerie Worth

This is a charming collection of valuable and usable rituals and magical techniques—all in rhyme! It is divided into four sections: The Materials of Wisdom, Inscription of Power, Thrice a Dozen Charms, and Ceremonies of the Year.

This book appeals to the imagination, as well as giving practical directions for the application or performance of numerous spells, charms, recipes, rituals, and more. These are based on familiar ideas and materials and are easy to carry out.

The Crone's Book of Wisdom relates powerful ancient practices, especially those of the old Nature Religions, to a modern appreciation of the world around us. It might even be seen as a kind of magical ecology, in which every manifestation of nature may be valued spiritually as well as cherished for its role in the environment.

In a world where nature is so often slighted or ignored, this book serves to heighten the reader's awareness of the magic lying beneath the surface, and the powerful ties that exist between mind and matter, even in modern times.

0-87542-892-4, 192 pgs., 5 1/4 x 8, illus., softcover $6.95

GLOBAL RITUALISM
MYTH & MAGIC AROUND THE WORLD

Denny Sargent

The concept of ritual and spirituality is common to all peoples, as the same archetypal powers dwell in the psyches of people everywhere. From Haiti to Egypt, *Global Ritualism* analyzes the common themes and archetypal symbols of higher ritual so that you can define how these archetypes play out in your own life. As you build a "global vocabulary" of such spiritual and magical symbols, you will be able to construct your own vibrant, living rituals—actively following a mythos that *you* create rather than one that has been given to you.

Let the subconscious language of human archetypes become your path to spiritual evolution and meaning. Become an "eclectic ritualist" and dare to live a more fulfilling life! Includes 300 photos of actual rituals as they are enacted around the world, including 16 pages of color photos.

0-87542-700-6, 256 pgs., 271 photos, 16 color pgs.,
7 x 10, softcover $19.95

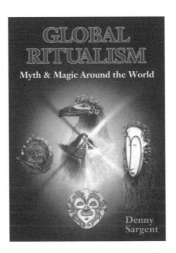

WHISPERS OF THE MOON
THE LIFE & WORK OF SCOTT CUNNINGHAM, PAGAN PROPHET

David Harrington & deTraci Regula

Scott Cunningham (b. 1956–d. 1993) authored more than 50 books in his lifetime, 15 of which lay the foundation for the non-institutional growth of modern Wicca. For tens of thousands of new Wiccans, their first magic circle was cast using his words of power. In addition, Scott also opened up a new understanding of positive, nature based magics such as herb, gem and elemental magic.

Whispers of the Moon combines Scott's unfinished autobiography with the added efforts of two of his closest friends. While the book traces his life and growth as a writer as well as a philosopher-magician, it also includes some of Scott's poetry, portions of letters, exposition of his personal philosophy and religion, and the complete text of his self-published pamphlet from 1982: *A Formula Book of Magical Incenses & Oils.*

With remembrances of Scott from many people, this book answers questions about his life, illness and death at age 37; his involvement in various Wiccan traditions; and his methods of research and discipline as a writer. What's more, it clearly demonstrates his importance as a prophet of modern-day nature religion.

ISBN: 1-56718-559-2, 6 x 9, 272 pp., photos, softcover $15.00

In a Graveyard at Midnight
Folk Magic and Wisdom
from the Heart of Appalachia

Edain McCoy

The rich folklore of southern Appalachia contains some of the most authentic and untainted Celtic magick still available in today's world. Now *In a Graveyard at Midnight* focuses on the magickal aspects of the lives of the mountain people, something no other single book about the region has ever done. For those who are interested in reclaiming and practicing natural magick, this book helps to recapture a dying art before it is lost forever.

Appalachian folk magick primarily concerns omens, portents, curses, cures, and protections, and is decidedly geared to non-material goals. In a place where shoes and secure homes have been luxury items, their magick focuses on intangible values: family and home, romance and children, health and dying. The title *In A Graveyard at Midnight* comes from the most prevalent of their folk magickal practices: casting a spell in a graveyard at the stroke of twelve.

In a Graveyard at Midnight is for those intrigued by Anglo-Celtic magick, for folk healers and folklorists, and for anyone with an interest in American folk beliefs.

1-56178-664-5, 240 pgs., 6 x 9, illus., softcover $14.95

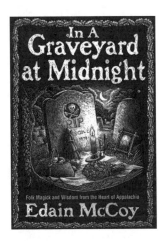

LADY OF THE NIGHT
A HANDBOOK OF MOON MAGICK & RITUAL

Edain McCoy

Moon-centered ritual, a deeply woven thread in Pagan culture, is often confined to celebration of the full moon. Edain McCoy revitalizes the *full potential* of the lunar mysteries in this exclusive guide for Pagans who honor the Old Ways and seek new ways to celebrate the Lady who is always young.

Lady of the Night explores the lore, rituals, and unique magickal potential associated with *all* phases of the moon: full, waxing, waning, moonrise/moonset and dark/new phases. Combined with an in-depth look at moon magick and suggestions for creating moon rituals that address personal needs, this is a *complete* system for successfully riding the tides of lunar magick.

Written for both solitary and group practice, this book is exceedingly practical and versatile. *Lady of the Night* reveals the masculine side of the moon through history and breaks new ground by showing how both men and women can Draw Down the Moon for enhanced spirituality. Pagans will also find fun and spirited suggestions on how to make the mystery of the moon accessible to non-Pagan friends and family through creative party planning and popular folklore.

1-56178-660-2, 240 pgs., 7 x 10, illus., softcover $14.95

To Stir a Magick Cauldron
A Witch's Guide to Casting and Conjuring

Silver RavenWolf

The sequel to the enormously popular *To Ride a Silver Broomstick: New Generation Witchcraft*. This upbeat and down-to-earth guide to intermediate-level witchery was written for *all* Witches—solitaries, eclectics, and traditionalists. In her warm, straight-from-the-hip, eminently knowledgeable manner, Silver provides explanations, techniques, exercises, anecdotes, and guidance on traditional and modern aspects of the Craft, both as a science and as a religion.

Find out why you should practice daily devotions and how to create a sacred space. Learn six ways to cast a magick circle. Explore the complete art of spell-casting. Examine the hows and whys of Craft laws, oaths, degrees, lineage, traditions, and more. Explore the ten paths of power, and harness this wisdom for your own spell-craft. This book offers you *dozens* of techniques—some never before published—to help you uncover the benefits of natural magick and ritual and *make them work for you*—without spending a dime!

Silver is a "working Witch" who has successfully used each and every technique and spell in this book. By the time you have done the exercises in each chapter, you will be well-trained in the first level of initiate studies. Test your knowledge with the Wicca 101 test provided at the back of the book and become a certified Witch! Learn to live life to its fullest through this positive spiritual path.

ISBN: 1-56718-424-3, 7 x 10, 288 pp., illus., softcover $16.95

To Ride a Silver Broomstick
New Generation Witchcraft

Silver RavenWolf

Throughout the world there is a new generation of Witches —people practicing or wishing to practice the craft on their own, without an in-the-flesh magickal support group. *To Ride a Silver Broomstick* speaks to those people, presenting them with both the science and religion of Witchcraft, allowing them to become active participants while growing at their own pace. It is ideal for anyone: male or female, young or old, those familiar with Witchcraft, and those totally new to the subject and unsure of how to get started.

Full of the author's warmth, humor and personal anecdotes, *To Ride a Silver Broomstick* leads you step-by-step through the various lessons with exercises and journal writing assignments. This is the complete Witchcraft 101, teaching you to celebrate the Sabbats, deal with coming out of the broom closet, choose a magickal name, visualize the Goddess and God, meditate, design a sacred space, acquire magickal tools, design and perform rituals, network, spell cast, perform color and candle magick, divination, healing, telepathy, psychometry, astral projection, and much, much more.

0-87542-791-X, 320 pgs., 7 x 10, illus., softcover $14.95

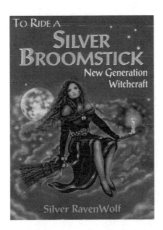